The BROKEN JOURNEY

E.M.WILKIE

THE
BROKEN JOURNEY

Aletheia Adventure Series Book 3

E M Wilkie

JOHN RITCHIE LTD
CHRISTIAN PUBLICATIONS

Copyright © 2014 by John Ritchie Ltd.
40 Beansburn, Kilmarnock, Scotland

www.ritchiechristianmedia.co.uk

ISBN-13: 978 1 909803 98 5

Written by E M Wilkie
Illustrated by E M Wilkie
www.aletheiabooks.co
Copyright © 2014

Cover illustration by Graeme Hewitson.
Interior illustrations are by E M Wilkie.

Unless otherwise indicated, Scripture quotations are taken from:
The Holy Bible, New King James Version®.
© 1982 by Thomas Nelson, Inc. Used by permission. All rights reserved.

To Bobby,

This third, snowy adventure was written for you.

"And as many as touched Him were made whole."

Mark 6:56

[King James Version]

PREFACE

This story is an attempt to help and encourage young readers to develop an understanding of the truth contained in the Word of God, the Bible. However, all characters, places, descriptions and incidents are entirely fictional and this adventure story is not intended to be a substitute for the teaching contained in the Bible, but rather an aid to understanding. The illustrations and allegories used in this story are not perfect; and therefore, whilst it is hoped that readers will benefit from the truth and lessons developed in this story, they must be urged to develop an understanding of Bible truth and doctrine from the Bible alone.

The author would like to acknowledge the invaluable help and advice of the following people who assisted in the production of this book:

M J Wilkie, R Hatt, A Henderson, and R Chesney;

and, in addition, Margareta, my youngest adviser,

whose comments I have so much enjoyed and appreciated.

Many thanks to you all.

Contents

Map Of The City Of Aletheia	i
Map Of The Land Of Err	ii
Chapter 1: The Attic Door	7
Chapter 2: Entry to a Fortress	17
Chapter 3: The Last Transporter	29
Chapter 4: Left Behind	43
Chapter 5: The Err Transport Monitor	53
Chapter 6: The Road to Topsy-Turvy	63
Chapter 7: Meddlers!	71
Chapter 8: Mr Tickle to the Rescue	81
Chapter 9: Topsy-Turvy Town	91
Chapter 10: A Desperate Escape	101
Chapter 11: The Damaged Snow-Beater	107
Chapter 12: Under Attack!	117
Chapter 13: The Call for Help	127
Chapter 14: The Mending of Josie	137
Chapter 15: Rescued	145
Chapter 16: The Mending Centre	155
Chapter 17: The Rescuer Enquiry	171
Chapter 18: The Plan of the Meddlers	187
Chapter 19: Flight to Aletheia	203
Epilogue	209
References	217

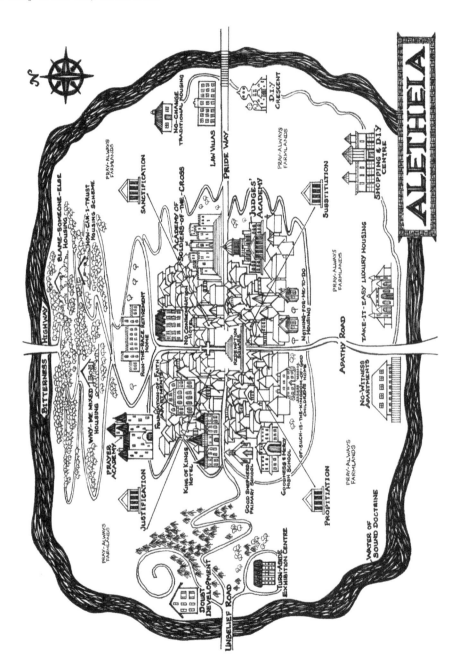

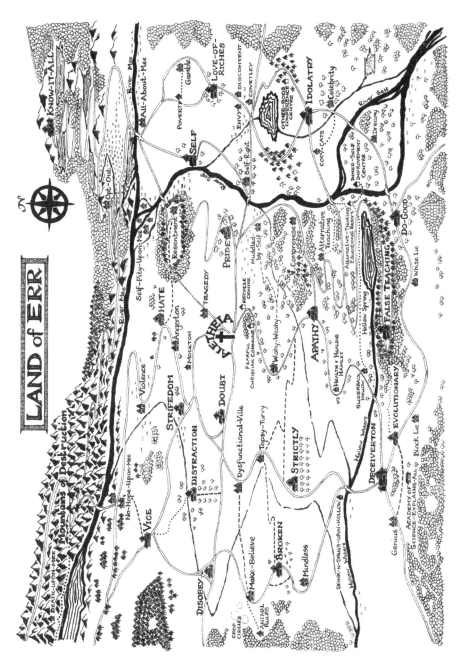

CHAPTER 1

THE ATTIC DOOR

It was the last day of school before the Christmas holidays. None of the children paid attention to schoolwork and for once their teacher, Mrs Bubble, didn't try to maintain the quiet she usually expected in her class. She didn't seem to hear the loud chatter. She didn't even notice the paper aeroplane that Alfie McPhee sent flying in the direction of Marigold Goody – who was the only child in the classroom diligently concentrating on the Christmas card assignment Mrs Bubble had set for that final afternoon of school. Mrs Bubble got up from her seat and began to stroll slowly around the room. She glanced at the splendid card that Marigold was making for her grandmother. Then she looked with interest at Jack Merryweather's unfinished Christmas card. It depicted a spooky shadow with cold, cruel eyes. The malevolent shadow was being hunted by a boy who held a large book that Jack had labelled 'The Bible'. Mrs Bubble didn't know what this had to do with the Christmas story, except, perhaps, that vague reference to the Bible. But Jack Merryweather was nothing if not surprising.

"That's an interesting card, Jack," said Mrs Bubble. "Who is it for?"

Jack looked at the card with a frown, as if he feared he hadn't got it quite right. "It's a Snare," he said. "It's for Timmy."

Jack's friendship with Timmy was something else Mrs Bubble considered surprising. She could not imagine how Jack, until recently small for his age and still scrawny and of no account to the bigger boys, had become friends with a big bully of a boy such as Timmy Trial. And, although Timmy had now left the school and was at the big High School in the nearby town, Jack Merryweather was still his friend.

"I'm sure Timmy will like it," murmured Mrs Bubble.

"It's to do with our adventure," said Jack.

"I see," said Mrs Bubble.

Of course, Jack knew that she didn't really *see* at all. Mrs Bubble didn't know anything about the city of Aletheia and the land of Err, or the adventure Jack and Timmy had had there in the summer[1]. Jack was wise enough to realise that Mrs Bubble would not understand even if he did tell her what had happened to him and Timmy during those few, fantastic days in Err. Sometimes Jack wondered if it had been real, and he knew that Timmy had begun to doubt it: which was why Jack had chosen to draw this particular scene on the Christmas card, to remind Timmy. Perhaps it would make Timmy think about the things they learned about the Bible and Christian life in Aletheia.

Since their adventure in the summer, Jack had returned to Aletheia only once. One night he had dreamt he was back in Aletheia with his friends; and in the morning his special spy watch was gone. He remembered he had removed it in Aletheia and left it there: so he knew the dream was real. He was desperately hoping he would go back to Aletheia and see his friends there, and even have another exciting adventure. But he didn't know the way. Adventures in Aletheia just happened; there didn't seem to be a great deal he could do about getting there.

"Here's your Christmas card, Jack." Marigold Goody placed a small envelope by his hand. The envelope was labelled 'Jack Merryweather' in very neat writing.

"Oh," said Jack. Now he wondered whether he should have written Christmas cards for *all* his class as his mother had suggested. Instead he had done a few hurriedly scrawled cards for his special friends – and there were certainly none for *girls*. "I didn't give you a card," said Jack to Marigold.

"That's OK," said Marigold.

"I expect you'll get lots from other people though," said Jack encouragingly.

Marigold's neat yellow pigtails moved on and she gave a Christmas card to Jack's friend, Alfie McPhee, who looked at her completely blankly. Jack wondered why girls seemed so much better than boys at Christmas cards and other such stuff.

"Happy Christmas, Jack," said Mrs Bubble. She was passing around the classroom again, this time handing out small, neatly wrapped gifts. She placed a gift on Jack's desk amongst the jumble of other things he was hastily stuffing into his rucksack as they all prepared to depart for the Christmas holidays.

"Thank you," said Jack. He fumbled for the small parcel his mother had instructed him to pass on to his teacher, only remembering it at that moment. Jack had insisted that Mrs Bubble didn't need a Christmas gift from him, but on this point his mother was adamant and now Jack was glad he had something to give her. It seemed a shame that Mrs Bubble should give all of them presents – even if they were disappointingly small – and not receive anything herself. Did Mrs Bubble know anyone at all apart from the people at school? Perhaps the gift his mother had insisted upon was the only present poor Mrs Bubble would receive this Christmas.

"Mum said to give you this." Jack found the squashed package and thrust it quickly at Mrs Bubble. "I think it's really from her," said Jack, "but I hope you like it."

"I'm sure I will," said Mrs Bubble. She was smiling her funny smile, as if Jack had just told his best joke and she was trying not to laugh. Jack wasn't entirely sure he had said the right thing about the Christmas gift, but he couldn't think what else he should have said.

"I hope you have a nice Christmas," he added, suddenly inspired.

"I hope you do too, Jack," said Mrs Bubble. "And don't have too many scary adventures!"

But with that Jack could *not* agree. An adventure, more specifically a return visit to the land of Err, and to his friends in Aletheia, was exactly what he longed for the most that Christmas: even more than all the presents under the tree.

Mum picked up Jack and his younger brother, Harris, from school and drove them home. Harris was in the youngest class; he didn't know much yet.

"Well, how was today?" asked Mum.

"I made snowflakes!" said Harris.

"Not real snowflakes," said Jack.

"Lots of snowflakes!" said Harris.

"I'm sure they're very nice," said Mum as she drove slowly past the crowds of excited children. "We'll have a look at everything you've both made when we get home. What did you do today, Jack?"

"Will it snow tomorrow?" asked Jack, not really paying attention and instead pondering the tricky problem of arranging snow at Christmastime.

"I don't think so," said Mum. "I'm afraid it might rain."

Jack looked out of the car window at the grey day which looked so decidedly un-Christmassy.

"It might snow on Christmas Day, Jack," said Harris.

Jack knew that Harris didn't really know that much so he didn't take any notice of his younger brother's opinion of snow on Christmas Day.

"Did you remember to give your teacher her Christmas present, Harris?" asked Mum.

"Yes," said Harris. "She said 'thank you.'"

"Did you give Mrs Bubble her Christmas present, Jack?" asked Mum. She sounded slightly wary; she had past experience of Jack's absentmindedness about the things he did not consider important.

"What was in the present?" asked Jack.

"Christmas cookies," his mother said. "I told you earlier. I hope you kept them safe."

Jack recollected the squashed package with the askew bow that he had handed to Mrs Bubble. He thought it was wise to remain silent on the details.

"Mrs Bubble gave me a present," said Jack.

"I got one from my teacher too!" Harris piped up.

"That's very kind," said Mum. She turned into the driveway of their home and parked the car. The two boys hastily grabbed their school rucksacks and ran for the house. Jack cheered up at the sight of the Christmas tree in the lounge, its lights all twinkling through the window into the gloom of the dull, winter day. And there were presents already wrapped and looking mysterious under the Christmas tree.

"Shall I put Mrs Bubble's present under the tree?" asked Jack, extracting the small, flat gift, the only item he considered was of any interest, from the jumble of his school rucksack.

"You could open it now if you like," said Mum.

Harris immediately tore the wrapping from the gift his teacher had given him. For Jack, the decision was more of a dilemma. Should he open Mrs Bubble's gift now, or should he save it for the unique specialness that was Christmas Day? In the end he decided to open it: largely on the basis that it was small, and that Mrs Bubble was unlikely to have given him anything that was all that interesting. But, when he removed the wrapping paper, he was surprised to discover a small book which was entitled 'Handbook for Adventurous Boys'.

"It's a book," he said. "To do with adventures!"

"How nice of Mrs Bubble!" said Mum.

"I got sweets," Harris said contentedly.

"I didn't know Mrs Bubble knew anything about adventures," said Jack.

That night, when dinner was over, Jack slipped away from Harris and went up the stairs to the very top of the house where there was only one door. It was the door to a big, dark, mysterious attic which was filled with old furniture and boxes and a great deal of unidentifiable jumble. Sometimes the boys played games such as hide-and-seek in the attic, or rearranged dusty items to make dens or to depict the scary shapes of monsters. But Jack wasn't thinking of playing tonight. He was on a secret mission to catch a glimpse of the big presents that he knew weren't yet wrapped and under the Christmas tree. He wouldn't look closely, for that would spoil the surprise; but the slightest peek at the shape of the presents, or just to see how big they were, that was all he wanted. He couldn't tell Harris, of course. Harris was too small to be entrusted with secrets and he would only tell Dad and Mum that they had found the secret hiding place for their gifts. No, this was something Jack needed to do alone.

He slipped through the attic door and felt for the light switch in the darkness. It wasn't a very good light, but it was better than nothing. He switched on the single dusty light-bulb and looked around the familiar clutter with some surprise. Since his last visit here someone had tidied the muddled space on the far side of the attic. Instead of the usual jumble of miscellaneous items and distorted shapes that were made out of lots of things that didn't really belong together, there were orderly shelves. Perhaps even more surprisingly, arranged neatly on the shelves, were dozens of pairs of sturdy walking boots. Jack tiptoed quietly through the more familiar jumble to the far side of the attic, avoiding the creaking floorboard he knew could be heard far below. He looked closely at the walking boots. He felt a sudden sinking feeling that Mum had been sensible and bought them all new boots for Christmas; perhaps he wouldn't get his new bike after all. But now that he thought about it, there were far too many pairs of boots for Christmas. And there was something oddly familiar about them, as if he had seen boots like that somewhere before …

In his preoccupation with the boots he almost missed the door next to the shelves. Jack wasn't aware until now that there was a door on this side of the attic and he certainly didn't know where it led. Perhaps it had been covered with clutter before; maybe there was another store beyond the door which contained secret, exciting Christmas presents that were not just boots.

Jack opened the door.

CHAPTER 2
ENTRY TO A FORTRESS

With considerable surprise, Jack peered into the strange passageway that lay beyond the attic door. He looked first one way, and then the other, up and down the long stone-flagged corridor. Of course, it didn't seem remotely possible that his house went on and on the way the passageway did, disappearing into mysterious darkness. But Jack was unaccustomed to questioning the unlikely; he rather enjoyed the unexpected. It was distinctly cold beyond the door, though, and Jack, realising he might not be dressed for whatever exploring lay ahead, looked around the attic for handy supplies. He put on a pair of the sturdy walking boots that were just his size, and then considered the pile of musty odds and ends which might be useful as additional clothing. The torn, stained tracksuit-bottoms that were part of the jumble of the attic were far too large, although he approved of their scruffy appearance, but the old patchwork quilt was conveniently adaptable. It was the blanket which his mum's Granny had knitted sometime in the dim and distant past. Jack had always been somewhat in awe of it, having the vague notion that she had *actually died* whilst wrapped inside of it. Still, it wasn't the time to be fussy about the blanket. Jack took it quickly from a corner of the loft, and, ignoring the musty smell, bravely wrapped the old quilt around his shoulders. Then he ventured through the attic door.

The very long passageway was all stone: stone-flagged floor, stone walls, and stone ceiling. It was just like the inside of a real castle and it echoed eerily as Jack started walking. To begin with there was no sight or sound of anyone. The castle – if it was a castle – seemed utterly deserted. Jack looked back to the tiny indent in the stone wall which led to his attic. If he kept going straight on he couldn't really get lost, could he? He would still be back before he was missed at home.

When he came to a junction, with other stone passageways leading in different directions and offering too many options, he no longer considered the distant dilemma of finding his way home again. There was no way he would return before he had explored a little further. And he had the oddest feeling unfolding in his mind that he was somewhere he very much wanted to be; somewhere he knew. The junction of passageways was not as deserted as the first part of his exploration, and very soon Jack saw a couple of people walking quickly along, following the sign which read, 'If in doubt, go this way for the Exit'.

"Uh, excuse me," called Jack.

"Yes?" said a harried-looking man. He wore a white lab coat over which was buttoned a warm, furry jacket with mismatching buttons. On his head was a knitted blue hat. He was accompanied by a clever-looking boy who wore thick-rimmed glasses and stared intently at Jack.

"Is that really your coat?" he blurted out. "I haven't seen one like that before!"

"Well, it's not a coat exactly," said Jack. "It's a blanket. I was in a hurry and just borrowed it." That didn't exactly explain much, but the boy didn't seem bothered.

"It looks pretty cool," he said, considering it from all angles.

"Uh, do you need something, young man?" asked the harried man. "It's just that I'm running late." He peered through his large glasses at the watch he wore on his wrist.

"I was just wondering where I am," Jack said politely.

"Where you are?" echoed the man.

"You're on the passageway that leads to the armoury," the boy said cheerfully. "At least I think that's where you've come from. Do you need to be somewhere else? Are you new around here?"

"Can you deal with this, Dusty?" asked the man anxiously. "I really need to be going…"

"Of course!" said the boy.

The man bustled away and the boy, Dusty, turned and grinned at Jack. "That's Mr Buffer, the Control Room Manager," he said. "He's worried because he hasn't done any Christmas shopping yet. He works too hard! But tonight he's hoping to get Mrs Buffer's Christmas present before the shops shut! Now, who are you?" asked Dusty.

"I'm Jack," said Jack.

"I'm Dusty," said Dusty. "I work in the Control Room whenever I can. It's completely awesome there!"

Another time Jack thought he would quite like to see the 'Control Room' – whatever it was. But for now...

"What building is this exactly?" he asked.

"It's the Academy of Soldiers-of-the-Cross!" said Dusty. "Where did you think you were?"

Jack knew he couldn't adequately explain that he had merely wandered through a door in his attic onto a random passageway in the mighty fortress in Aletheia. For now it was enough to know that his best hopes had been realised and that he was, really and truly, back in Aletheia again!

"Are you supposed to be going on the Christmas mission?" asked Dusty. "You'd better hurry if you are – I think Lieutenant Faithful and Private Wallop are the last to leave and they're very nearly on their way! I know, you see," he added confidingly, "I've just been looking at the Central Mission Detector and a few minutes ago I could see Bourne and Harold were still in the Academy and just about to depart for Broken! Bourne's in charge, you see. He's made sure everything is ready here and in Err for the Christmas missions."

"Oh," said Jack, trying to process the information and also recognising with relief the name of Harold Wallop. "Could you... would you mind taking me to Harold?" he asked.

" 'Course I don't mind," said the obliging Dusty. "Come on! It's this way!"

On their journey through several passageways, down a couple of narrow, winding staircases, and around several unexpected turns, Jack learned a bit more about Broken and the Christmas mission that was taking place there. According to Dusty, there were Christmas missions taking place all over the land of Err. "I know, you see," said Dusty earnestly, "because I can see everything that's happening on the Central Mission Detector in the Control Room. Everyone is in place for the Christmas missions – all apart from Bourne and Harold and you. You're the very last to set out for Broken."

If 'Broken' was actually a place it sounded pretty strange. "Why is the town called Broken?" asked Jack. He remembered that in the land of Err the towns and plants and trees and other things took on the characteristics of the people. And sure enough...

"It's called Broken because everything is broken there," said Dusty. "The mission is to tell the people of Broken how the Lord Jesus can make them whole again. Apparently they try to mend themselves, but I've heard the results of their own fixings are pretty weird! I guess you'll see when you get there!"

Jack tried to imagine people and things that were broken, all trying to find out how to be put back together again. He was glad the folk from Aletheia were going to tell the broken people about how the Lord Jesus could make them whole[2].

There was only one open door on the deserted passageway ahead. Light spilled from the door into the corridor and, as they approached, they could see a man checking the contents of a large rucksack, clearly preparing to depart. Dusty didn't hesitate. "You're only just in time!" he said, and then he called, "Harold! You've got another passenger!"

Harold Wallop quickly entered the passageway from the open door. "Are you coming with us after all, Dusty?" he said.

"No, not me!" said Dusty. "I can't leave the Control Room! No, it's Jack here…"

When they reached Harold he gave a startled exclamation. "Well I never!" he said. "Hugo and Henry were quite certain you would come back in time for Christmas! They said they had, uh, met up with you a few weeks ago. And here you are! Only just in time too!"

"That's what I said," said Dusty.

"Bourne!" Harold called over his shoulder. "We have another member for our mission!"

Another man appeared in the study doorway. "Hello, Dusty!" he said.

"No, not me!" said Dusty, rather enjoying his involvement in helping the boy with the colourful blanket who was clearly one of Harold Wallop's friends.

"This is my cousin, Lieutenant Bourne Faithful," said Harold. "And this young man is Jack Merryweather of the famous escapade to rescue Timmy Trial!!"

Lieutenant Bourne Faithful was a fierce-looking Rescuer. His appearance was daring and bold and he had a scar across his cheek. He was older than Harold, and Jack noticed that he had *two* gold stripes on the shoulders of his uniformed jacket. But Bourne also had a twinkle in his eye and he was looking at Jack and his blanket with amusement. For the first time Jack wondered whether the musty quilt had been a wise choice.

"The boy who faced the Snares!" said Bourne with a grin. "Just what we need for our mission!"

"You and Timmy and Hugo and Henrietta became somewhat famous after your escapade with Mr Weighty's Rescue Craft and the Snares," explained Harold.

"Did you really face Snares?" asked Dusty.

"It wasn't exactly like that," said Jack, surprised that in the adventurous and unexpected land of Err his travels and encounter with the Snares should be considered noteworthy.

"Well, we're certainly glad to have you with us," said Bourne. "The famous boy who defeated Snares might even be able to take on the Meddlers!"

Jack had once seen a Meddler on a poster. It was a tiny flying imp with a rather nasty face. It didn't look half as scary as the Snares.

"Did you forget your coat, Jack?" asked Harold, also eyeing with interest the curious patchwork quilt.

"Well, I didn't really expect to be here, you see," said Jack. "I just borrowed the quilt to come and explore."

"Ah," said Harold.

"I never quite know how it works when you come here," remarked Bourne. "I've heard about it, of course, but it's still a puzzle to me."

Jack didn't know how it worked either, but he wasn't inclined to question it; he was only glad he was back.

"Well, I can lend you a jacket," said Harold. "You'll need a warm one for the snow!"

"I don't really want the blanket anyway," said Jack, unconcerned at the fate of the patchwork quilt which was really proving rather embarrassing. "It just happened to be in the attic when I left."

"Well, that explains everything," said Bourne with a smile.

"Actually, I think someone died in that blanket," Jack confided to his friends.

For some reason Jack's candid admission amused Harold and Bourne.

"Uh, if you want to leave it with someone while you're away, I'll look after it for you," said Dusty.

"You can have it!" said Jack generously. "You can keep it for showing me the way!"

Jack wasn't completely sure it could be spared from the attic at home, but there was no way he was going to tell Dusty that. He was only pleased that he had something to give Dusty for the trouble he had taken. Jack had heard his mother say something about the musty quilt having 'sentimental value', but as he wasn't sure how valuable sentimental value was, he was more than happy to give it away. He could always save up his pocket money if *sentimental* value proved to be especially expensive.

"Thanks, Jack," said Dusty earnestly. "And wait until I tell the others at the Of-Such-is-the-Kingdom-of-God Children's Home where I board that someone *actually died in it* too!"

Dusty departed happily with the knitted patchwork blanket draped around his head and shoulders, completely unconcerned how very odd he looked.

"You'll need armour, of course, Jack," said Bourne briskly, ushering Jack inside the study. "We've got plenty here so we can kit you out without going to the armoury."

"I see you're already wearing your armour boots, Jack," observed Harold, as he handed Jack his body armour and belt.

Jack looked down at the boots he had found in the attic only a short while before. Were they really armour boots? He didn't question how that could be, instead he hurried to put on all the pieces of the armour of God[3]. He knew that Christians in Aletheia wore real armour when they left the safety of the city and went into the land of Err. He knew he needed to be fully protected against the creatures of Err that were ready and waiting to attack a Christian who did not equip himself as the Bible said he should. Of course, the Christians in his own country needed to wear the armour of God too; but Jack had learned that, where he lived, you needed to put the armour on in your mind. It wasn't less real; it just couldn't be seen.

The last thing Jack did was put his Bible carefully into the pouch at his side. This was a weapon against which no enemy could stand. The Bible was the sword of the Spirit, the Word of God[4]. It was the weapon that God had provided for Christians, to protect and guide and defend them.

At last they were ready to go. Bourne closed his study door behind them. "We have to take security measures even here," he explained. He removed his Bible from the holder at his side and pressed it into a book-shaped indentation in the old timbers of the door. "We've had

an invasion of Meddlers in Aletheia, and one was even spotted just a street away from the cross!"

"But Meddlers couldn't get right up to the cross, could they?" asked Jack, following the two men down the stone passageway. The clump of their boots echoed on the floor and Jack's words seemed to echo around them too: *Could they?...could they?...could they?...* Could the wicked creatures of Err invade even Aletheia and get to the safest place in the land – to the cross?

"No," said Harold. "Although Meddlers would like to, they can't meddle with the cross. *Nothing* can meddle with the cross!"

"Of course, Meddlers can't usually survive anywhere even close to the cross," said Bourne, leading them down yet another long, echoing corridor with another high, vaulted ceiling, and stone walls. "Meddlers cause problems and break people apart, but there is no room for strife at the cross because the Lord Jesus brings lasting peace to everyone who believes.⁵"

Jack breathed a sigh of relief. The thought of any of the wicked creatures of the land getting close to the cross was too awful to contemplate.

If Christians weren't safe close to the cross, they weren't safe anywhere.

CHAPTER 3
THE LAST TRANSPORTER

It was beginning to snow when Harold, Bourne and Jack left the shelter of the massive stone Academy of Soldiers-of-the-Cross. It was a bit of a shock to Jack just how cold it was and how much snow lay in heaps on the ground outside. Paths had been cleared, but fresh snow was once more quickly covering the walkways.

They went down the wide steps, and passed the towering Christmas tree that was shining and twinkling by the huge entrance doors. The sky was almost completely dark, and the thick clouds of the snowstorm obscured the stars and blotted out the light of the moon. The city was shrouded in darkness, huddled against the coming storm; only the cross in the centre of the city was somehow still visible to all who looked. In Aletheia you could never be lost: you could always see the cross.

Bourne and Harold murmured together about the coming storm and the state of the roads that led to Broken; but Jack, who hurried after them between the mounds of snow, was perfectly content. He did not worry about the snow, the Transporter, the equipment, the prayer-cover for the mission, the wicked creatures of Err, and the many other things that the two Rescuers had been trained to think about. He was absolutely content to go with them wherever they might choose to take him, even to a place with a name as strange as Broken. And his satisfaction with arrangements only increased when he spied the huge Transporter waiting for them by the Academy.

Jack had never seen anything like that Rescuer Transporter. It was a gigantic caravan sat on big flat runners, like an enormous, ungainly sledge. It had the words 'Rescuer Transporter' painted in big white letters on the shining black side, and out of the top of it poked something that looked just like a chimney!

"It's the last Transporter to leave Aletheia for the Christmas mission," remarked Harold. "The others are already being used in the missions across Err."

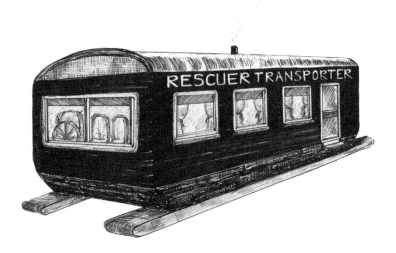

Jack wouldn't have cared how many Transporters were in Aletheia or in the entire land of Err – as long as he got to ride in one of them.

"It's not the latest model," said Bourne, "but we'll be warm and snug enough!"

"It's very nice," said Jack, feeling he needed to attempt some expression of his feelings of utter joy at the sight of it, but knowing words were completely inadequate for the huge contraption.

Bourne knocked on the door in the side of the Transporter. To Jack's surprise, a small, round man with a jolly face and a big, bushy, white beard opened the door. For a fleeting moment Jack imagined they had stumbled across Father Christmas, but he was glad he did not make that observation aloud to his friends, for Bourne Faithful simply introduced the jolly old man as, "our driver, Mr Tickle," and ushered them inside out of the snow.

Mr Tickle was really a most remarkable man. He exactly suited his name and seemed at any moment about to give way to sudden, infectious bellows of laughter, really without much provocation at all. It was, thought Jack, just as if someone invisible tickled Mr Tickle, and Mr Tickle just couldn't help the chuckles that rumbled from his considerable tummy. He was most interested to meet Jack and openly gleeful that he had been given the honour of driving the last transport vehicle on the Christmas mission, including driving the organiser of the entire event: Lieutenant Bourne Faithful.

Bourne and Harold were somewhat less impressed by the fact that Mr Tickle, of all the drivers of the fleet of various rescuer vehicles, had requested, and been granted, the honour of driving them. Jack, naturally, didn't care who drove them. This wonderful machine could have gone anywhere in the world and it wouldn't have mattered much to him. He spent some time just gazing around the interior of the big caravan-type space, hardly able to believe his eyes.

There was a wide, cushioned bench of deep crimson running the considerable length of the Transporter, with soft, colourful cushions spread here and there; there were thick crimson curtains at all the windows, with golden ropes and tassels to tie the curtains back. At the driver's end of the Transporter there was a small kitchen area with cupboards and a kettle and pots and pans hanging from the ceiling. In the very middle of the strange house-on-wheels there was a big wood-burning stove with a chimney that really did go straight through the ceiling as Jack had imagined he had glimpsed from the outside. Just now there was a lovely fire of hot coals and crackling wood keeping the inside of the Transporter wonderfully cosy; Jack could see the red glow of the flames through the small glass doors of the wood-burner. And, as if that wasn't enough, opposite the long bench-seat there were actually three beds, screened with curtain hangings, already made up and waiting just for them.

"I heard there were three of you coming," Mr Tickle explained with a rumble of his infectious chuckle, "so I've got the beds all ready for you, sirs!"

"Very good," said Bourne. He didn't seem inclined to keep Mr Tickle talking, and he and Harold took their seats on the cushioned bench. Bourne quickly extracted a neat table from under the bench, set it up, and spread out some maps and papers.

Mr Tickle invited Jack to sit in the front of the Transporter for a while and Jack, understanding that Bourne and Harold, who were deep in discussion, were unlikely to need him, was more than pleased to join Mr Tickle. There was an extremely large steering wheel, of a size befitting the monstrous Transporter, behind which Mr Tickle sat, his short, chubby arms barely able to reach all the controls around him. Jack did not recognise many of the buttons and switches, which were of various shapes and sizes and colours. But he did remember a few of the gadgets from his last adventure in the land of Err and the glorious ride he had then enjoyed in Mr Weighty's Rescue Craft[1]. There was the Mission Detector that all Rescuers had in their various vehicles – a flat screen that came in different sizes and showed a map of the land of Err, gave directions and information about the towns around and about, and showed the location of people who were praying for help. When the Rescuers saw a person praying for help in Err, they could go and rescue them and guide them to the cross.

"I've been a driver for the Rescuers for forty years!" said Mr Tickle. "I wasn't much good at books and learning at school, all I ever wanted to do was drive! Of course, I'm not *just* a driver! Oh no!" He sneezed and then burst into prolonged and merry laughter while the Transporter, which already seemed to take up the entire road, wavered dangerously from side to side. "We almost hit the bridge!" chortled Mr Tickle when he had gained some control over himself. "We could have been swimming in the Water of Sound Doctrine by now! Not that that would do us too much harm, oh no! You can never get too much of the Water of Sound Doctrine!"

Jack thought he heard an exclamation from Bourne and things falling to the floor; he imagined all of Bourne's maps and plans spread over the entire Transporter because of Mr Tickle's precarious driving.

"Have we left Aletheia?" asked Jack. He knew the Water of Sound Doctrine encircled the entire city. The only way in and out of Aletheia was over one of the four bridges that led to, and from, the city. The water was the only safe drinking water in the land of Err; it represented the whole truth of the Bible and Christians were in danger if they stopped drinking it, or if they changed or altered or added to the balanced Water of Sound Doctrine. Jack peered at the Mission Detector screen and saw a white dot moving cautiously down Apathy Road, south out of the city of Aletheia. At the side of the screen there was a warning flashing in scrawled writing that looked as if someone had just scribbled a note. 'It's snowing!' the warning read, 'Please drive carefully!'

"It doesn't need to tell us it's snowing!" said Mr Tickle, laughing. "We can see that, can't we?! In fact, we can't actually see anything else! Ha Ha!"

Jack thought the flashing warning on the screen about driving carefully might have been useful, but Mr Tickle seemed to know what he was doing, even if he didn't look at the road much and instead fiddled happily with the various switches and gadgets by which he was surrounded.

"Yes, we've left Aletheia," said Mr Tickle, "the only safe place in Err," he added, suddenly sober. "You can't trust anything in the land of Err, young man!"

Jack knew that of course, but it was difficult to believe they had entered dangerous territory while they were riding in this magnificent machine, warm and snug and secure from everything around them.

"Of course," Mr Tickle remarked, "the snow isn't so bad here. Everything is a bit lazy on Apathy Road, even the snow! It falls more slowly here than in some parts of Err."

"Is the snow different in different parts of Err?" asked Jack, intrigued with this idea.

"Oh, dear me, yes!" said Mr Tickle. "Whatever do they teach you at school these days?" He didn't really give Jack a chance to explain that he wasn't taught anything about the land of Err and the city of Aletheia in his school. Despite Mrs Bubble's Christmas gift of a book about adventures, Jack was still pretty certain that Mrs Bubble hadn't ever heard of Aletheia or Err. "As I said, the snow in the Apathy area is slow and lazy. It's probably the easiest place to live in the winter. But the snow elsewhere in Err? Well, it depends on the town, doesn't it? If you're close to Hollow Spring and areas like False Teaching it can be anything – hollow, for example. Whatever it is it's always somewhat unexpected: it plays false, you see. I suppose it's a bit like a joke gone wrong!" and Mr Tickle chuckled for a moment, enjoying the thought. Then he continued, "If you're somewhere like Drink-n-Drugs-Upon-Hollow it can be red or blue or all the colours of the rainbow!" Mr Tickle once more gave way to prolonged guffaws of laughter. "And where we're all going, the town of Broken, well, it's very sad." He was suddenly sober and sighed deeply. "The snow there is broken, the same as everything else," he said.

"Broken?" asked Jack, exceedingly puzzled at the description. How could *snow* be broken?

"Broken," agreed Mr Tickle tragically.

"Uh…*how* is it broken exactly?" asked Jack.

"How?" Mr Tickle repeated. "Just broken, young man. Around the town of Broken the snowflakes are maimed and not pretty like the ones you see elsewhere; you might get bits of snowflakes falling, fluttering, limping, like they've got broken wings; you might get snow that is stained and dirty; and you might get big snowballs falling and bashing everything around! Oh, everything is broken in Broken!"

Jack was still struggling to picture a town where everything was broken. "How are the, uh, people broken?" he asked.

"The poor people," said Mr Tickle sadly, and he sighed without further enlightening Jack. But it didn't seem in Mr Tickle's nature to give way to melancholy and it quickly passed. "There is one town I would like to see," he confided. "And that's the town of Topsy-Turvy. It's so…" But with the thought of the town of Topsy-Turvy Mr Tickle began to laugh again, and it was some time before he regained control over his rumbling chuckles and wiped his eyes. "You know what I mean," he said to Jack. And Jack, who knew nothing whatsoever about a town called Topsy-Turvy, learned nothing further of the matter.

Mr Tickle was quite right when he told Jack that he didn't just drive the Transporter. In fact, he did just about everything there was to do about the Transporter: he cleaned and mended and repaired; he made the beds and pulled the curtains; he kept the wood-burner going in the winter and the ice maker in the summer; and he cooked for his passengers. When Jack realised this last job – that of chief cook – was the responsibility of the driver of the Transporter, he decided he might need to rethink his own suitability for the job. He watched in awe when Mr Tickle left the controls of the slowly ambling Transporter – which really was built much more for comfort on long journeys than for speed – and began frying sausages and bacon and heating lovely bread rolls for supper. The Transporter continued to trundle onwards with no one at all at the controls, although Jack saw Bourne go quietly to the curtained section at the front of the vehicle and check that Mr Tickle had left it on the right auto-setting. It seemed that Bourne and Harold did not have unlimited faith in Mr Tickle's driving abilities, although there was no doubt that he was a very well-meaning companion.

Mr Tickle served them sausage and bacon rolls and hot tea and returned to the controls of his beloved Transporter. Bourne and Harold left their maps and plans and joined Jack on seats close to the cosy wood-burner.

Bourne questioned Jack about his family and his home, and Jack tried to explain the differences between his home and what he knew of the way Christians lived in Aletheia. Bourne was most interested.

"I'd like to visit your country," he said. "Is that possible, do you know?"

"I don't know," said Jack. He remembered how, when he returned from his first adventure in Aletheia, he and Timmy and their friends, the Wallops, had gone through the same door – but only he and Timmy had ended up back near the village school of Steeple-Bumpton again.

"Well, we'll try to think of a way," said Bourne.

Jack was very pleased – and somewhat perplexed – at the thought of a big Rescuer warrior like Bourne Faithful, with his scars and fierce appearance, coming home with him. But, on the other hand, there was Timmy.

"You might be able to help my friend Timmy," he said.

"How *is* Timmy?" Harold wanted to know. "We haven't seen him back here yet."

Jack tried to explain how hard it was to be a Christian when you were growing up – when all the things a Christian needed to be and do seemed so invisible and difficult and sometimes seemed to make so little difference; especially when Timmy's big friends, who weren't Christians, enjoyed things that seemed to be so real and exciting.

"I don't think I've explained it very well," Jack concluded, eating the final piece of sausage on his plate and glancing surreptitiously to see if there were any more. But Mr Tickle's frying pan was now definitely empty.

"I think I understand," said Bourne. "It's hard for Christians here too. It's too easy to take your eyes off the cross and start focussing on the things around you that might seem so much more appealing."

"Yes, that's it," said Jack.

"As Christians, we must learn to walk by faith, and not by sight,[6]" said Bourne. "That's what makes the difference."

Jack wasn't sure what he meant, but he was glad that Bourne seemed to know the answers. Somehow it must be possible for him to help Timmy.

It felt very late when Jack got into the cosy bed that Mr Tickle had prepared for him. When the thick curtains were drawn around him, shutting out most of the light, and the wind howled around them, Jack thought of Timmy and asked God to help him, wherever he was. He lay awake for a few minutes listening to the quiet, comforting murmur of Bourne's and Harold's voices as they continued to talk about their mission. He heard the faint crackle of the fire and the cheerful, off-key sound of Mr Tickle as he hummed a hymn.

And then, despite the fact that Jack was quite certain he was not tired at all, he fell fast asleep.

CHAPTER 4
LEFT BEHIND

Jack woke with a start and sat straight up in bed. It was not clear what had woken him. Around him there was darkness and stillness and silence. He sat very still, listening intently. There was no doubt that the Transporter had stopped and he was alone. Had they reached their destination, the town of Broken? Very faintly, through the howl of the wind, he could hear the sound of voices from somewhere beyond the window. Harold and Bourne and Mr Tickle seemed to be outside.

Jack got out of bed and looked through the thick curtains that surrounded his bed. There was a faint glow of light from the wood-burning stove which had ceased to crackle but still shed warmth. Jack slipped his feet into his armour boots and put on Harold's big jacket. He left the rest of his armour. He would just take a peek outside to see what was happening.

Cautiously he opened the side door of the Transporter and looked out into swirling, blinding snow. The wind was fierce and cold as Jack stepped out of the Transporter. His boots sank into the snowdrift that was quickly accumulating outside. He had never seen so much snow! He heard the sound of voices close by and thought he saw a faint light. He could hear disjointed words such as "Meddler attack", a cheerful voice (which he figured was the ever-optimistic Mr Tickle), saying the words "soon mended", and the more grim tones of Bourne or Harold – who sounded quite alike through the storm – saying something about "lack of prayer cover" and "unprecedented snow". Jack took a few steps through the snow in the direction of the voices.

"Naerly thare," he heard someone say close by. He took another step in the direction of the distorted words. The shriek of the cold wind was muddling the words and voices. They didn't sound like normal voices at all.

"Soun bee om yoor wey," Jack heard another voice say.

He was puzzled. He seemed to be getting close to Harold and Bourne and Mr Tickle, and yet he seemed to be going in the wrong direction too.

Something other than the snow appeared to be tangling in his hair and swirling around him. "Hello!" he called. "Harold? Are you there?"

"I'n hear!" Jack heard quite distinctly close by.

Immediately he plunged through the snow. Harold was somewhere very close by. But he had reached the faint outskirts of a wood and was standing amongst scattered trees that showed dimly through the darkness and the swirling snow. And then Jack knew for sure he had gone in the wrong direction, despite the voices close by that sounded just like he imagined Harold or Bourne might sound through the snow and the howling wind.

Jack knew he must get back to the Transporter. Something weird was at work here and he had gone the wrong way. He suddenly recalled the words "Meddler attack" and wondered for the first time if it were those creatures he could hear calling and misleading him. He turned and quickly made his way back through the darkness, trying to follow the only light he could see, which was feeble and uncertain through the storm. He knew now that he should never have left the safety of the Transporter, and certainly never left it without all of his armour on. It was an elementary rule in the land of Err: a Christian never ventured into Err without all their armour on, no matter how safe it seemed.

And then, through the darkness and the wild call of the wind, Jack heard a sound which was at once welcoming – and terrifying. It was the sound of the Transporter and it was once more on the move. He was too late! Harold and Bourne and Mr Tickle would think that he was still safely in bed behind the thick curtains he had left closed; they were leaving without him!

"Hey!" yelled Jack. "Wait! Wait for me!"

"Twoo lote!" said a voice mockingly.

"Yoo'we bean left behond!" said another.

"Wee trickled yew!" said a third.

"Who are you?" asked Jack, standing still in the snow, his heart thudding as he realised his awful predicament. He was left behind in the land of Err, without his armour, lost in a snowstorm in the freezing cold, with all the creatures of Err somewhere around and about him. He was glad for his armour boots; at least his feet didn't feel cold; but he wasn't sure what good his armour boots were against these strange, shrill, reedy voices that came from every direction and even from thin air. Did these creatures fly? Were these the Meddlers that had apparently "attacked" the Transporter and made it break down?

There was shrill mocking laughter in the air around him. Or was it only the shriek of the wind…? Certainly it was nothing like the warm, comforting laughter of nice, old Mr Tickle, and Jack felt he would have given anything to be back in the safety of the snug Transporter, away from this darkness and the swirling snow and the voices that mocked and caused the churning, frightened feeling inside his tummy.

"Whoo r wee?" a voice from the darkness echoed his question.

"Yew donnt noo whoo wee r?" said another.

"Pour ickle bouy!"

Jack could make no sense of the dozens of voices. He understood what they said, he knew they were creatures of Err – probably Meddlers who deceived and mocked and told tales and lies and caused strife wherever they went – and he knew, above all things, he could not trust them to help him; not in the least. He tried to think very hard what to do: but it was difficult without the helmet of salvation[3] to soothe his fears and to keep his mind focussed on what the Lord Jesus would want him to do. And it was hard to think when the voices of the creatures riding the wind continually mocked and muddled him. He tried not to panic; he tried very hard to overcome the mortifying feeling that he might actually cry.

He moved to the shelter of a big tree nearby and tried to shut out the mocking voices. He pulled up the collar and hood of Harold's warm jacket and buried his nose into the soft fur. He thrust his hands deep into the pockets to keep them warm. He was so glad he had put on Harold's jacket and it comforted him to think of his big, dependable friend who had also, perhaps, worn this jacket when he faced the foes of Err. Jack's fingers closed on items in the big pockets and he wished he had a light to see what he could feel there. First he pulled out three bars of what he thought must be chocolate. That was handy. Jack knew you couldn't eat just anything in the land of Err. It must be safe food that was good for a Christian. There was a sudden, lightning-swift movement from close beside him and one of the precious bars of food was suddenly whisked from his hand.

"Hey!" he shouted, more angry than frightened as the bar vanished into thin air.

"Hay!" returned the shrill, mocking voice of the creature that had robbed him.

"Hay! Hay!" they jeered.

Jack thrust the other bars of chocolate – or whatever they were – deep into the pockets of the jacket and safely out of reach. He felt some folded paper in the pocket but did not dare to remove it and could not, in any case, see it without a light. In the other large main pocket he felt soft gloves which he knew would be far too big for him but which might be useful nonetheless. But there was nothing else to help him.

He sank back against the tree, defeated.

"Pour ickle bouy!"

"Ickle bouy 'lone fourewer!"

"Ickle bouy cry boo-hoo!"

The voices continued and Jack, feeling very much afraid that he might sit down in a snowdrift and give in to the creatures' taunts and cries, tucked his head further out of the swirling snow into the warm fur collar of Harold's old jacket and frantically began to pray. He wasn't sure what to say, so he started with the obvious: he asked God for help to find his way through the storm and to shelter or safety – wherever that might be. And as he prayed, Jack was aware of the creatures around him beginning to lose interest and drift away.

"Knott fare!" he heard one say sulkily.

"Ickle bouy donnot wanted two pley!"

"Go away," said Jack, emboldened by the defeat he sensed around him.

"Yew go awey!" said another sulkily.

Suddenly they sounded like spoilt children, not like frightening creatures at all.

With sudden inspiration, Jack withdrew one hand and felt along the zip that fastened the jacket. Sure enough, there was a secret pocket, safer than the others. Eagerly he opened it and felt the strange package inside. He didn't know how he could have missed it before, but, feeling the utmost joy and relief, he withdrew from its safe hiding place a small Bible. It did not, of course, matter how small the Bible was: the size of a Bible didn't matter. It was the Word of God and it was the most powerful, the most comforting, the most effective weapon a Christian could ever wish to have.

As he withdrew it, the light of the Bible spilled around him, overcoming the darkness and scattering the flying imps he could now see swarming around him. With shrill cries of terror and frustration the Meddlers, which had plagued and tormented him, fled helter-skelter into the snow and melted away.

There was sudden stillness. Not only had the Meddlers vanished, but the wind that had howled so unrelentingly began to drop and the falling snow began to slow. A faint light appeared in the sky as the moon peeped cautiously from behind big, dark clouds. The fierceness of the storm had passed. Feeling emboldened by the comfort of the Bible, Jack eagerly searched the remaining pockets of the jacket – which appeared to have many hidden compartments – and unearthed two small sticks, a crumpled note in scrawled writing which looked private, a map of the town of Pride (which Jack didn't think was likely to be particularly helpful), and the two remaining bars of food which he could now read in the light of the Bible, each labelled 'Chocolate Energy Bar'. Most interesting of all was a small, compact screen.

He was excited with the small screen. Could it be a mini Mission Detector which might show him the way? He pressed the side of it, the middle of it, the back of it, the top of it, the bottom of it, all the

while anxiously watching for a flicker on the screen that might bring it to life. There was nothing. It was small and dark and still, and yielded absolutely no information at all. But it reminded Jack that other Mission Detectors, such as the one on the Transporter, would show he needed help if only he started to pray.

And so Jack started to pray.

He began to walk slowly too, feeling his way from the shelter of the trees, away from the wood and back to where he imagined the road would be. He felt so much better when he prayed. It was as if he was wearing the helmet of salvation, even though he had left his behind on the Transporter. Jack remembered old Mr Duffle who lived in Aletheia, and how great things happened when he prayed. Mr Duffle had prayed for him and Timmy when they were trying to escape the Snares[1]. And when Mr Duffle prayed, strange, inexplicable things happened. It wasn't that Mr Duffle was a special type of Christian who had the power to make extraordinary things happen when he prayed, it was just that Mr Duffle had learned that God could do great and wonderful and powerful and impossible things: and so Mr Duffle had the faith to ask God for greater things than other people did.

Jack held the small Bible in his hand, following its unwavering light as he walked through the deep snow. He had put on Harold's gloves too, and as long as he kept praying he felt brave enough to keep going through the cold and the darkness.

And onwards into the unknown.

CHAPTER 5
THE ERR TRANSPORT MONITOR

The snowstorm continued to abate and soon only a few harmless flakes of snow drifted slowly from the night sky. The moon, emboldened by the passing of the storm, crept from its hiding place and shone brightly over the snow-covered land.

Jack looked around him. He had, after all, managed to reach the road. He could see it clearly in the moonlight, and there were even the very faint tracks of what might have been the Transporter cutting a line through the smooth surface of sparkling white.

The road ahead sloped gently downwards and Jack knew from previous experience in the land of Err that all the roads out of Aletheia lead downwards. If you wanted to find your way to Aletheia and the cross you must climb upwards. And then you would reach the hill which was crowned by the city of Aletheia, with the cross, the safest place in the entire land, at the very centre.

Jack hesitated as he glanced up the road to where he could faintly see the cross on the top of the hill in the far distance. He had a choice. He could start walking up Apathy Road and back to Aletheia, or... he glanced down the road. Not far ahead, clear in the moonlight, was a small shelter. He didn't know how he hadn't seen it before, but he

had certainly prayed for a shelter from the storm. It seemed right to
at least investigate it.

Jack began to walk towards the shack at the side of the road. As
he approached it he was most surprised to hear the sound of voices.

"A bus to Steeple-Bumpton?" a man was saying in disbelief. "Is that
a joke? I've never heard of such a place! Steeple-Bumpton indeed!"

Jack was utterly amazed. He hurried forward. Steeple-Bumpton?
He had *certainly* heard of Steeple-Bumpton even if the unknown man
hadn't! Steeple-Bumpton? Why, that was his home village! He lived

in Steeple-Bumpton! But what was someone doing asking about it in the middle of the land of Err?

Jack reached the shack which looked a bit like a large bus shelter in his own village – expect that all the sides were enclosed. They were made of mismatched materials – wood and plastic and metal, and there was a makeshift door in the side. Jack opened the door. On the inside, the hut was nothing like a bus shelter at all. For one thing, it contained a fire blazing from a brazier. Seated beside the fire was a large man in an extremely scruffy armchair. But it was the tall boy standing by the man who gave Jack the biggest surprise of all.

"Timmy!" he cried. "Timmy! It's me, Jack!"

Timmy Trial turned quickly and stared at Jack. "Well!" he said, looking with astonishment at Jack. "Well, I've never been more glad to see you in my life, Jack!" He thumped Jack on the arm and Jack laughed aloud, so pleased, so amazed, so glad he was to see his friend again.

"And where do *you* need to go, young man?" asked the man in the scruffy armchair, fixing Jack with a disgruntled stare. "I only volunteered for this shift because I thought I might get some peace! Anyone who wants to travel tonight is nuts! But instead of peace and quiet…" He gestured at the two boys, struggling to understand what kind of strange reunion was taking place in his remote shelter on such a cold and stormy winter night.

The big man had certainly come prepared for peace and comfort. He had a frayed paperback book on a small table by his chair, beside which was an open box which contained sandwiches and squashed cakes and a jumble of other edible things. There was also a flask of something hot that was steaming on the table. A faded cushion was propped behind the man's head, and his large feet were stretched in front of the fire that blazed in the brazier, with the big toe peeping from a hole in one of his socks. It was such a strange scene to stumble across that Jack would not have believed it but for the fact that they were, after all, in the middle of the land of Err: just about anything could happen in Err.

"We need to get to the town of Broken," Jack said in answer to the man's question about where he needed to go. Jack was very certain of this despite Timmy's evident surprise.

"Well, at least that's a real place," the man said, shifting his considerable bulk in the chair, which squeaked and groaned in protest.

"A real place?" echoed Timmy. "Jack, are you sure…?"

"Yes," said Jack. "We need to get to Broken," he repeated to the man who very much resented the interruption. Jack saw the badge on the man's dirty, frayed uniform. The badge read 'Err Transport Monitor', and 'Happy to Help'. There was also some information about Err Transport on a worn, stained poster on the side of the shelter. Jack looked at it and read the words 'We tell You the Way', which seemed to be the Err Transport slogan.

"How do we get to Broken?" asked Jack.

"Alright! Alright! Hold your horses!" the man said crossly. He obviously didn't bother with the 'Happy to Help' bit of his badge. He reached for a large, black rectangular box which lay on the table by his book. "I don't know what the hurry is," he grumbled, "especially going to a place like Broken, where everything is broken! No one in their right mind goes there! And at Christmastime too! The roads are…" He shook his head very dubiously and pressed a button on the side of the black box with a large, grimy finger.

"Jack!" Timmy whispered urgently. "What's going on? What is this place called *Broken*? Are we really back in Err?"

"Got a couple of likely lads here, Merv," the Err Transport Monitor said into the black box. The box crackled and popped. "You there, Merv? Over." The man sighed as he glanced at the two boys who had invaded the not-so-salubrious quarters he preferred to enjoy in solitude.

"Hearing you, Plod," a voice came through the crackles and Jack looked at the Err Transport Monitor with interest. He really did look as if his name should be Plod.

"They want to get to Broken. Over."

There followed some garbled words from the man Merv which neither Jack nor Timmy understood.

"Naw! Not the Christmas Party at Drink-n-Drugs!" Plod exclaimed at the end of the incomprehensible response from Merv. "You're at the party just now?...Naw, they want to get to the town of Broken!...Beats me!...Yeah, I reckon they're pretty crazy too! I told them everything is broken there...No Err Transporters going that way, you say?..." There was more crackling and popping as Merv once more relayed a message only Plod seemed to understand. "No Err Transporters going to Broken," Plod interpreted for the boys. "Mind you, that's not surprising, is it? No demand for that route, see?"

"*Transporters?*" Timmy muttered to Jack. "Do you know what he's talking about?"

Jack nodded, feeling very wise. He only wished they could find the wonderful Rescuer Transporter and be safe with Harold and Bourne and Mr Tickle.

Plod finished his entirely unproductive call to Merv on the crackling black box and looked gloomily at the two boys. "No Err Transporter to Broken," he repeated, which they certainly knew by now. "Why are you going there anyway?" he asked suspiciously. He poured some hot, foul-smelling liquid from his flask into a cup and leaned back in his creaking chair, waiting for an answer.

Timmy looked at Jack. He had no idea what Broken was or why they were going there.

"There's a Christmas mission from Aletheia going to Broken," explained Jack.

"Christians?" the man asked warily.

"Yes," said Jack.

"Why are you wasting your time on broken people?" The man took a long drink of the hot liquid and then burped without apology and patted his tummy.

"I think that's *why* we're going to Broken," said Jack. "To tell the people there that the Lord Jesus came to mend broken people and make them whole again.²"

Plod looked at them in silence and then took another long drink of the dark, dubious-looking liquid. He didn't seem to have a ready answer to Jack's simple explanation. "Well, if you want to meet broken people that's certainly the place to go!" he grunted.

"But how do we get there?" asked Jack.

There was no one else to ask and, since Plod was an Err Transport Monitor, Jack thought it reasonable to suppose he ought to know how to get around Err.

Plod hoisted himself out of his chair with a sigh of annoyance. "I don't suppose I'll get any peace until you two are on your way to Broken!" he said. "Although exactly how you'll get there I really don't know. But see here…" He placed his grimy finger on the grubby map which was stuck to the unreliable walls of the shelter. "That's where we are now," he said, and Jack looked closely at the spot on Apathy Road, somewhere between the towns of Wishy-Washy and Apathy. He had hardly travelled any distance at all in the Transporter. "The most direct route to Broken is across country to the town of Topsy-Turvy, and then across country to Broken." Plod's dirty fingernail tracked the faint path which showed across country from roughly where they stood, to Topsy-Turvy and beyond. "Of course, the path is several inches deep in snow," said Plod. "I don't know how you'll get there," he added, "you'll be drowned in snow! And if you do get close to Broken there aren't many signs, they're all broken too!"

"What other umm…other vehicles are there around here?" asked Timmy.

"*Vehicles!*" scoffed Plod. "Hark at him!" he said. "I don't think there's a vehicle that will get you to Broken! An Atob isn't likely to be travelling there, I think a Snow-Beater is about the only thing that will get you close to Broken and there aren't many of those around! *Vehicles* indeed!"

"I don't know why *vehicles* should be so odd to a *Transport Monitor*," Timmy muttered to Jack as Plod took another long swallow of his dark drink. "And what on earth is a *Snow-Beater?*"

"No idea," muttered Jack in return.

Both boys were familiar with the Atob that Plod had mentioned. An Atob was a three-wheeled vehicle that took you from A to B. They had both seen one of these on their previous visit to Aletheia. It was a small, slightly odd contraption, with seats facing front and back. In Err it was customary to have armchairs for seats in vehicles and, as Jack had just experienced, in some transport they had comfy beds too.

Plod stopped drinking and placed another log on his brazier which immediately crackled and blazed. Then he sank back into his chair and picked up his book, staring pointedly at the two boys. "Well, if there's nothing more I can do to help?" he said. It was obvious he wanted them to leave him in peace with his hot drink and his blazing fire and his tatty book. Jack wondered if he was going to stay there all night. Perhaps he even lived there.

"Oh, I guess we'd better go then," said Jack.

He opened the door of the fragile shelter and a blast of cold, icy air hit him.

"He's not exactly *happy* to help," Timmy muttered, thinking of Plod's 'Happy to Help' badge.

Plod had already opened his book and put his large feet close to the fiery brazier. "Shut the door behind you," he said.

"Happy Christmas!" said Timmy sarcastically.

And the two boys left the warmth of Plod's singular shelter, and faced the cold, winter darkness together.

CHAPTER 6
THE ROAD TO TOPSY-TURVY

The two boys left the warmth of the Err Transport shelter and quickly discovered the side road which led from Apathy Road to Topsy-Turvy – which was not actually so hard to find since a vehicle of some description had recently taken that very snowy turn. They trudged side by side through the snow, glad to have the tracks of a vehicle to follow in the bright, clear moonlight. As they walked they talked about the strange events of the last few hours.

Jack told Timmy about going through the attic door and finding himself in a passageway in the Academy of Soldiers-of-the-Cross. He explained about the subsequent journey with Harold Wallop and Bourne Faithful, and about being left behind when the Meddlers confused him with their lies and strange voices and the Rescuer Transporter went on its way.

For his part, Timmy had a straightforward story to tell. He had decided to go and see Jack. "I thought I hadn't been to see you much," he said somewhat sheepishly, and Jack knew he was thinking about the way he had neglected Jack and his other Christian friends, and spent time with his friends who weren't Christians instead.

"That's alright," said Jack.

"My dad dropped me in Steeple-Bumpton just down the road from your house," continued Timmy. "I was walking up the street to your house when there was suddenly a *massive* snowstorm!"

"Like the snowstorm here," Jack remarked.

"Exactly like here," said Timmy, "because I think that it probably *was* here!"

"You mean that in the snowstorm…"

"When the snowstorm came I walked right into Err and I was on Apathy Road!" said Timmy.

"Wow!" said Jack.

"Anyway, I saw a shelter…"

"Plod's transport shelter!" Jack said eagerly.

"But to start with I thought it must be the bus stop near to your house!" said Timmy.

"So that's why you were asking Plod the way to Steeple-Bumpton!"

"Exactly," said Timmy.

Jack laughed. It was impossible to put into words how strange it was that they were in Err once more and had met in this unexpected way.

"But I'm glad to be here again," said Timmy. "At least, I am as long as we don't get too badly lost!"

"I was afraid you might have forgotten about…well, all about the

Lord Jesus and being a Christian," Jack admitted as they walked onwards through the snow.

"I think I did forget a bit," said Timmy. "But I don't think I'll ever *not* be a Christian, even if I'm not very good at it."

"No," agreed Jack, "I don't think that can ever happen, because once the Lord Jesus has saved you, you can't be lost again, can you?'"

"I looked up a verse about that," said Timmy. "I was afraid I might not be a Christian anymore, because I don't think I act like one."

"I don't think God can ever lose hold of someone who belongs to Him," said Jack.

"No," said Timmy. "No one can ever take you out of His hand. That's what the verse in the Bible said[7]."

They walked in silence for a time, and when it seemed they had walked a long, long way and they were both beginning to feel weary, the boys stopped walking and took stock of their surroundings. They were still following the track made through the smooth sparkling snow, optimistically hoping that it led to the strangely named town of Topsy-Turvy. All about them was a barren landscape of glittering snow, where there was not a house or a shelter or a soul in sight, and no one was close enough to help them. It was just as well Timmy had dressed in his winter jacket and had gloves and good boots, and for the first time Jack realised that Timmy was also carrying a big rucksack strapped to his back.

"What have you got in your rucksack?" asked Jack.

Timmy shrugged slightly carelessly. "Just my school stuff, and…Oh! I almost forgot. I've also got a Christmas cake that my mum made for your mum! So we've got food, Jack! And here I was thinking that we might starve or freeze to death in the snow!"

Jack laughed. "*And* we've got these energy bars of chocolate," he said. "Harold must have left them in his pockets."

"Well, they must be OK to eat, then," said Timmy. Timmy had good reason to remember the dangers of the food of Err. Only the food produced by the Pray-Always Farmlands and watered by the Water of Sound Doctrine was safe for a Christian to eat in the land of Err. Everything else was contaminated with things that would muddle or confuse or weaken a Christian so that they could not defend themselves against their enemies in Err.

"I've got a Bible," said Jack, removing it from the safety of the small, zipped pocket where he had placed it. He had not thought he needed its light as the light of the moon shed bright rays over the snowfields. But now that he held the Bible once more in his hand he realised that the golden light that spilled from its pages was a different kind of light altogether[8].

"I've got a Bible too," said Timmy, rummaging in his rucksack and removing it. He held it cautiously in his hand, as if he were afraid it would not show the light that spilled from the pages of the Bible that Jack held. But strong, golden rays shone unhesitatingly from its pages and Timmy looked glad and amazed.

"I wasn't sure it would be like this," said Timmy.

Jack understood that Timmy had lost confidence in his Bible and in how real and powerful it really was.

"And I think the Bible is warming me up too!" exclaimed Timmy. "It really is warming me up!"

Jack concentrated on the Bible he held in his hand. Harold's gloves which he wore were far too big to warm his hands effectively but the Bible really did begin to make his fingers tingle, and wonderful warmth was spreading from them and making him feel comfortable for the first time on that slow journey across the snowfields of Err.

"If we always give the Bible the right place on our journey, perhaps it will not only guide us, but it will give us warmth and comfort too," said Timmy.

Timmy sounded so grown-up and wise as he said it. But Timmy was a little sad too, as if he realised he hadn't always given the Bible the place it should have in his life. Timmy didn't feel he was a very good Christian and Jack didn't know what to say to help him.

The boys divided one of Harold's energy bars between them. Ahead of them lay the faint track that snaked away across the snow into the darkness beyond. There was not a light, not a sound, and, apart from the marks left by the vehicle which had showed them the way, and the faint tracks of a rabbit which had long since returned to the shelter of its burrow, there was no sign of life around them.

"Do you actually know where we are?" asked Timmy.

"Not exactly," replied Jack. He hoped Timmy wouldn't blame him if they got lost and didn't find their way home in time for Christmas. How long could they stay in Err without time moving on back home? He had horrible visions of them just reaching Plod's unwelcoming shack again in a few days' time, just in time for Christmas; and it was not clear how they were both to return home again anyway. There were so many unknown elements to an adventure in Err.

"Are you sure there isn't anything else in those jacket pockets that might help to show us the way?" asked Timmy.

"There's only this," said Jack, and he removed the small, black screen from the inside pocket. "I can't get it to work though," he said.

Timmy carefully examined the screen, pressed all the buttons that Jack had pressed, shook it up and down, and then shook it from side to side, and there was nothing, not even the smallest flicker, from the small, black screen. "That's a pity," Timmy said with a sigh.

They walked onwards because there wasn't really anything else to do. The energy bar helped them to start with – they felt refreshed when they had eaten it. But when the snow once more began to fall, and the moon slunk behind thick black clouds, and the wind sprang up and blew blinding, icy snow into their eyes, with increasing weariness both boys trudged into the nothingness ahead.

They wondered where they were going.

And what on earth they should do.

CHAPTER 7
MEDDLERS!

Just when they thought they couldn't walk any further, Jack and Timmy entered a patch of woodland where there was some shelter from the storm. They stopped beneath a large tree with wide spreading branches which were sagging under snow. Snowflakes continued to fall and swirl around them, but at least there was some shelter from the worst of the wind. With a shaky hand, Jack removed the second precious energy bar from the big pocket in Harold's jacket and silently handed half to Timmy.

"What shall we do?" asked Jack. He supposed that it was really his fault they were lost and alone in the wilds of Err in the worst snowstorm he had ever seen. He had never thought there could be too much snow, not ever. But now even he wished it would stop and that they might find some shelter from the cold.

Timmy ate the half energy bar in silence, his back against the big tree. Then, "What about that screen in your pocket?" he asked. "I'm sure there must be a way to make it work. We've just got to find the right way!"

Jack slowly removed the screen from the inside pocket. "Hey!" he cried, "watch it!" as the small screen flipped crazily from his hand and went flying into deep snow.

Timmy made a dive for it, so did Jack, both of them fumbling for it in the snow.

"I was going to give it to you!" said Jack. "You didn't need to snatch it!"

"Snatch it!" retorted Timmy, "I didn't snatch it! You deliberately dropped it into the snow!"

"I did not!" Jack flared up. "Why would I do that? You know full well I didn't!"

"I know nothing of the sort!" exclaimed Timmy. "And it's not funny! Stop laughing or I might just have to make you!"

"I'm not laughing!" said Jack. "As if this is even a tiny bit funny! Ha, Ha! *Not!* You're the one who's laughing!"

"If you think *I* think this is funny…!" began Timmy, at last grabbing hold of the small screen which seemed to have taken on a life of its own.

"Stop!" said Jack. "Stop, Timmy!"

"Who are you to tell me…!" Timmy began angrily. "This whole disaster, us being lost here, was all *your* decision! You *insisted* that we go to the town of Broken! And I've just about…!"

"Wait!" urged Jack. "Just stand still and be quiet!"

Timmy was so surprised and furious at this last command from Jack that he actually did just that. For a moment he was still and both boys stared at each other as the strange laughter, which they had thought was each other, continued in the air around them.

"It's the Meddlers!" exclaimed Jack.

"Meddlers?" echoed Timmy.

"Ooh, big bouy and ickle bouy fight!" said a strange, shrill voice that Jack at least recognised.

"What-what…?" Timmy stuttered in utter bewilderment.

"It's Meddlers," said Jack. "Remember? Just like the ones I described to you when I got lost from the Rescuer Transporter. They cause trouble and strife. We mustn't let them…!" A big snowball smacked onto the top of his head and Jack yelled in annoyance. Another snowball smacked into Timmy and he turned around and glared at Jack. Jack held his empty hands open. "It's the Meddlers," he said. "Don't let them…!"

"Bouys want nicey snowballs?" mocked a shrill voice.

"I see one!" exclaimed Timmy, and thrust his hand out into the air and the swirling snowflakes, only to find it empty, while mocking laughter echoed around him. "I saw it!" said Timmy. "An ugly, little flying imp! Oww! Stop that!" He made another dive for the Meddler that had just pinched his ear, but they were far too quick and there were too many of them to catch or defeat. They taunted the boys and encouraged them to come after them, knowing their efforts would only be in vain.

"Stop!" said Jack. He was trying to remember how he had defeated the Meddlers the last time, but it was hard to think straight with the lightning-fast creatures constantly poking and pulling at them, and snatching at the small screen that Timmy had thrust deep inside his pocket.

"They don't like the Bible!" said Jack. But they were so beset by the awful flying imps that it was suddenly impossible to retrieve their Bibles. "We should never have put our Bibles away," Jack said miserably. He wasn't quite sure how it had happened, but at some point on their journey they had returned their Bibles to their pockets.

"I think we should pray," said Timmy. A Meddler had pinched one of his gloves and it was even now flying high above them and dumped onto the branch of the big tree, far beyond their reach. Snow showered around them, over their heads and going down their necks.

"Yes, pray," said Jack, wondering how he would explain the loss of both of Harold's nice thick gloves and also of the folded note in the pocket of his jacket. He hadn't read the note, he thought it looked private; he only hoped it wasn't important.

"Ooh," said the shrill voice of

a Meddler. "Ickle bouy has nicely lovey lettar!" And Jack looked up to see Harold's note clutched in the spindly, surprisingly strong, hand of a tiny Meddler.

"Do you mean to say these miserable creatures can actually read as well as speak?" exclaimed Timmy. He had lost his other glove too and both boys battled to keep hold of their Bibles in their pockets, and of the small screen which seemed so important even if they couldn't make it work.

"Lettar two 'Arold," said a Meddler.

"That's private!" Jack shouted at them.

"'Rivate! Oooh!" said the Meddlers, gathering in swarms around the piece of paper and carrying it to the nearest branch of the tree in order to read it.

"What is that letter?" Timmy asked Jack, taking a swipe at a nearby Meddler and for once managing to cuff it soundly on the back of the head. It probably wasn't worth his trouble though; it only meant that a dozen Meddlers descended on him, squealing in anger and renewing their attack.

"No idea what it is," said Jack, panting as he too came under renewed attack. "But it's obviously a private note to Harold!"

"Silly-billy 'Arold lovey-dovey!" said a Meddler. Apparently they could not read particularly well as they didn't seem to make much more of the letter than that, and Jack was uncertain whether they had just made up the bit about it being a love letter. He liked to think that Harold was above all that kind of stuff.

Amidst the continued attack, with both boys trying to stop the Meddlers undoing their shoe laces and continually trying to get into Timmy's rucksack and into all their pockets, Jack thought gloomily of trying to explain to Harold how his note, perhaps a treasured letter which was actually from a *girl*, had been carried off into the wilds of Err in the hands of a small, scrawny Meddler.

But it was one thing dealing with *one* of the small, flying imps, and quite another dealing with a whole band of them.

"Jack!" yelled Timmy, as several Meddlers attacked the pocket where the small screen was clutched in his hand.

"Pray!" yelled Jack in return.

"We need help, Lord God," said Timmy. "Please!"

Jack wished he could remove his Bible from his pocket. That would help, he just knew it. But he remembered lessons he and Timmy had learned in Err on their previous visit, about using the Bible in the right way and quoting the right Bible verse for the right moment. "Can you think of a verse from the Bible?" Jack cried to Timmy.

Around Timmy, the Meddlers continued to swarm, concentrating on the small screen still in his pocket. The Meddlers seemed to think it was of importance too. "Please, Lord!" Timmy prayed aloud. "We don't have the right words to say, but please help us to be rid of these Meddlers…!"

Strangely, amazingly, there was a brief respite from the storm of Meddlers that seemed to have multiplied every minute since the boys had first become aware of them. They were simply everywhere – in the branches of the trees, now and again showering snow on the two boys or calling insults or swooping down to join the fray of swarming, flying imps below. But suddenly, at Timmy's desperate prayer, they seemed to slow and falter, and Jack could hear hisses of disappointment. In the temporary lull of the Meddlers' attack a verse from the Bible came into Jack's mind:

"You will keep him in perfect peace whose mind is stayed on You,[9]" Jack quoted aloud from the Bible.

There was a collective howl from the Meddlers who sat in their dozens in the branches of the trees. They threw snow down on the two boys in disgust, but then whole groups of them took flight and vanished into the still falling snow.

"It's working!" cried Timmy. "Do you know any more verses, Jack?"

Jack only wished he did. But wait, last year his Bible Club teacher had taught them some verses from the book of Proverbs in the Bible, and there was one about being a meddler…

"It is honourable for a man to stop striving, since any fool can be a meddler,[10]" Jack quoted the verse he had learned, unsure how successful it might be.

Timmy laughed in triumph as, with many mutterings and complaints, Meddlers began to fall away from his pockets and stop pulling his hair and ears and filling his mind with strife and anger and annoyance. "Please, Lord," he prayed, "despite our weakness and failing, please help us to be honourable and remove us from this meddling!"

That seemed to be the final straw. The last few Meddlers that were clinging to the boys and hovering in the hope of doing more mischief at last fell away, and quickly vanished into the night, as if it had all been a dream.

Timmy sank to the ground beneath the tree. He didn't seem to realise he was sitting on snow, snow that had been flattened by all their trampling around in their fight with the Meddlers. Jack sat down beside him, and they both leaned back against the broad tree. Sometime during the Meddlers' attack the snow had stopped falling and the moon now shone brightly on the snow-covered wilderness around them.

"I'd forgotten about the power of prayer," murmured Timmy.

"We should pray for help now," said Jack.

"Yes," said Timmy. "We should have prayed before we set out from

Plod's ridiculous shack. We shouldn't have minded what he might have thought about it... But, anyway, we can pray now."

"Remember Mr Duffle's prayer sticks?" asked Jack, referring to their previous adventure in Err when old Mr Duffle's prayers had proved so powerful when Timmy had been captured and taken away by the awful Snares[1].

"I haven't prayed much recently," Timmy admitted wearily. "And if you stop praying, well, somehow it's hard to start again."

Jack was silent. He wasn't sure what to say to comfort his friend. He wished Harold Wallop or Bourne Faithful were there to advise Timmy. But he didn't know if they would ever see them again; nothing seemed likely at this point.

"I don't think God holds it against you," said Jack hesitantly. "I think He forgives, the same way He does when we get saved and become a Christian."

"Yes," said Timmy. "I was looking for Bible verses about that too, and I found a verse which says that if we confess our sins God is faithful and forgives us.[11]"

"Yes, that's right!" said Jack. "It's sort of like when we're saved and become a Christian, when we ask God to forgive all our sins and He does that because of the Lord Jesus! Of course, you only need to be saved once, but..."

"But when we sin again, God will forgive us again if we ask Him to," agreed Timmy. "I just wish I knew how to really behave like a Christian."

They were both weary and dispirited but took it in turns to pray for help. They even prayed for other lost people, that they might be rescued too. But answers seemed so far away on the remote, lonely snowfields of Err. When they had finished praying, Timmy got slowly to his feet and reached inside his pocket. "I think I know what might make this work," he said thoughtfully, and withdrew the small, black, blank screen. He gazed at it in silence and Jack also got to his feet, waiting for Timmy's idea.

"Where is the Bible that was in Harold's pocket?" asked Timmy.

Jack withdrew the small Bible and handed it to Timmy. Timmy held the Bible in one hand, and the screen in the other, and then carefully placed one on top of the other.

They fitted like a hand in a glove and suddenly, with no other prompting, the screen made a peculiar, but reassuring, buzzing sound, as if it had just woken from sleep.

Now the screen could show them where they were in the snow-covered land of Err.

To the boys' astonishment, they were no longer lost.

CHAPTER 8
MR TICKLE TO THE RESCUE

"I thought it would work!" exclaimed Timmy, whilst Jack gaped in surprise at the small, black screen which now had the words 'Welcome to the Mission Detector: Latest Voice-Activation Software' scrawled in white across what had been blank, lifeless darkness.

"How did you think of that?" asked Jack.

"It was what you said about access and security for the doors around the Academy of Soldiers-of-the-Cross," Timmy explained. "You had to fit the Bible to the door in order to gain entry or make it secure. And the Bible and the screen in Harold's pockets – they're meant to fit together, sort of like a password!"

"Who is this?" a mechanical voice came from the small screen and Timmy almost dropped it in surprise.

"Uh, it's Timmy Trial and Jack Merryweather," said Timmy.

"Not Harold Wallop," the machine commented. It didn't seem like a question but Timmy thought he had better answer it anyway.

"Uh, no, it's not," he said. It felt a bit odd talking to a screen, but he supposed that Harold had the latest in Rescuer technology in this small Mission Detector and somehow it responded to voices.

"Detector already determined not Harold Wallop," the machine droned, and if it could have put expression into its monotone syllables, Jack was certain it might have been sarcastic.

"Password question being processed," the Detector announced.

Timmy and Jack glanced at each other anxiously.

"Where was Jesus Christ, the Saviour of the world, born?" asked the Detector in its dead-pan expressionless voice.

"In Bethlehem," both boys answered promptly.

"Bible password question is too easy," the machine commented. If it could have grumbled or asked a harder question the boys were quite certain it would have done just that.

"Preparing owner's password question," the Detector intoned. "What is Harold Wallop's mother's name?"

Jack and Timmy looked at each other with a slight hesitation. But thankfully it didn't last long. They remembered spritely Mrs Wallop very well and they mouthed the answer to each other, fearing to upset the Detector with a discussion about it. Since they both agreed, Timmy said, "Daisy?" in a slightly questioning tone.

" 'Daisy' is correct," said the Detector. "Passwords complete. How can I help Timmy and Jack?"

"Can you tell us where we are?" Timmy asked eagerly, whilst Jack nodded his agreement. And then they both looked at the small screen that now had 'Searching for answers' scrawled across it with buttons flashing at the side. It seemed an easy question for the Detector because it didn't take long to answer.

"Current location eighteen miles south-east of Topsy-Turvy; nearest town is Topsy-Turvy," the machine announced.

Still all those miles to walk! Jack realised they should have asked the scale of the map in Plod's dirty shelter before they set out on this hopeless journey of snowdrifts and Meddlers and not much else that was of any use. They had hardly travelled any distance at all and Topsy-Turvy was far beyond their reach that night.

"Umm, is there any shelter or a house of some sort between here and Topsy-Turvy?" Timmy asked desperately.

"Processing question about shelter and house-of-some-sort," the machine announced, and began flashing and flickering.

Perhaps Timmy's description of a 'house-of-some-sort' confused the Mission Detector as there was a period of silence. Then, "No shelter until Topsy-Turvy," the Detector said succinctly. "Check for transport?"

"Yes!" cried Timmy and Jack at once, glad the Detector had prompted them.

"Processing transport request," said the Detector in its strange mechanical voice, but Jack could almost imagine kindness in its tones; impossible, of course, but then, this was a Rescuer's Mission

Detector and both he and Timmy knew from past experience there was a whole lot more to these machines than you might think.

"Transport for Timmy and Jack already on the way," announced the Detector matter-of-factly.

"On the way?" exclaimed Timmy. "What do you mean?"

There was a pause as the Detector tried to understand the question.

"Rescuer Transport en route to current location," said the Detector. "Prayer request already alerted Rescuers."

"Someone's coming to help us!" cried Jack.

Timmy looked at once incredulous and hopeful. "But how can that be?" he asked. "How on earth would anyone know...?"

But before he had finished his question the Mission Detector interrupted in mechanical tones that Jack imagined were somewhat exasperated. "Bees how on earth?" intoned the Detector. "Searching for answer."

Jack giggled and Timmy's face suddenly lost the grim uncertainty of moments before; it seemed too incredible to be true, but both boys were beset with the feeling of wonderful relief that the Mission Detector must be right and that help, Rescuer help, was really and truly on the way to them.

"Due to topsy-turvy nature of plants in vicinity of Topsy-Turvy town, bees do not thrive. Nearest location of bees is town of Strictly."

Jack giggled again. "It can tell us all about Topsy-Turvy!" he whispered to Timmy.

"Why is the moon so bright here?" Timmy asked the small screen in his hand.

"Processing question," said the Detector.

Both Jack and Timmy looked up at the moon that was, indeed, strangely bright. It was a fierce, white light. Not like the golden warmth of sunlight: it was cold and cast deep shadows all around them. They were approaching a strange part of Err, and, when they looked more closely at the trees in the weird light, they realised that the branches seemed to take the appearance of roots, and that the bigger shrubs around them seemed sort of, well, upside down.

"Topsy-Turvy environment is topsy-turvy," the machine announced.

"Makes sense," Timmy whispered to Jack, trying to keep out of reach of the sound sensors of the Detector.

"In Topsy-Turvy and surrounding locality, the sun and moon appear to trade places. The moon shines like the sun, and the sun shines like the moon," said the Detector. "Effect on health of population of Topsy-Turvy: extreme sleep deprivation; advisable for Rescuers to wear eye-protection at night to stop tiredness and ultimate madness."

"Wow," said Timmy. "A town that is really and truly upside down and opposite to what it should be. Can you imagine how crazy that might be?"

Through the bright moonlight they faintly saw something approaching them across the fields of snow. Somehow they had no doubt that it was coming to rescue them.

"Uh, thanks for your help," said Timmy to the clever Mission Detector, and then he slipped the small screen into his pocket.

Their prayers had been answered. Help was on its way.

The smooth-running, strange-looking contraption headed the final distance across the snow to the shelter of the trees where Jack and Timmy stood.

"Well, well!" said a hearty voice, and there was a burst of sudden warm laughter across the cold air. "Here I am! Don't just stand there! Come on in!"

"Mr Tickle!" gasped Jack. He didn't know what or whom he had expected, but Mr Tickle had never featured in his mind as their Rescuer! Timmy had of course heard of Mr Tickle from Jack when he recounted his earlier adventures of this same, strange, endless night.

"He looks like…"

"Father Christmas," concluded Jack. "I know."

What was even more bizarre was the fact that Mr Tickle was

driving the most marvellous-looking sleigh, just as if he really and truly was Santa Claus. But it wasn't exactly a sleigh such as you might see on a Christmas card: this contraption did have big, wide runners, but it also had a solid roof, and windows which glowed with light and warmth. At the front of it was a big snow plough, but instead of just shoving the snow out of the way, this vehicle simply gobbled up the snow, heated it up, melted it, turned it into steam, and ran smoothly and speedily on steam as long as there was snow enough for it to gobble.

"It's a Snow-Beater," said Mr Tickle proudly, reading the puzzlement in the boys' faces. "I've borrowed Welly and Sanny Stable's Snow-Beater to come and fetch you. Wellington and Sanity Stable are the nearest Outpost Rescuers in this part of Err, you know."

"Oh," said Jack.

"Right," said Timmy.

None of it made much sense, but they were not inclined to question their timely and most welcome rescue, and the appearance of Mr Tickle at their precise location was not, after all, particularly difficult for him to explain.

"Well, you prayed, of course!" said Mr Tickle. "And that showed us where you were on the Mission Detector! You gave us such a fright, my boy, when we discovered you weren't asleep in your bed and that we'd lost you!"

Mr Tickle escorted them into the interior of the Snow-Beater and Jack and Timmy looked around them in awe. There were deep seats along both sides of the large cabin, and cushions and blankets too, and in the centre, similar to the Transporter but on a much smaller scale, there was a compact wood-burning stove which was crackling with a cheerful fire.

Mr Tickle gave the boys something hot to drink which warmed them deep inside. For the first time in hours – and Jack didn't know how many had passed since he and Timmy left the shelter of Plod's shack – both boys felt warm and secure.

"You can sleep on the seats," said Mr Tickle. "I'll try not to disturb you with my singing!" he chuckled as he took his seat at the controls which were numerous and looked far too complex for Mr Tickle to manage. Jack sank onto the seats at one side of the Snow-Beater and Timmy took the other side. They both took off their boots and jackets and pulled thick blankets right up to their ears. Jack wondered if Mr Tickle was any safer driving the Snow-Beater than he had been driving the Transporter. But then he pictured the fields of snow by which they were surrounded and figured that even old Mr Tickle couldn't do much harm. It wasn't as if they could even get stuck in snow drifts: because, incredible though it seemed, the Snow-Beater would simply eat its way through them all!

Timmy was already snoring softly, as the Snow-Beater, with a curious hissing sound, went smoothly on its way.

Jack closed his eyes.

And soon he, too, was sound asleep.

CHAPTER 9
TOPSY-TURVY TOWN

The bright moon was high in the sky when both boys woke in the stillness of the warm Snow-Beater. It appeared to be bright daylight outside, but it was still night. In Topsy-Turvy so many things were the opposite way to what they should be. The sun shone dimly in the day, shedding a poor, half-hearted light on the town so the people of Topsy-Turvy were sleepy and inattentive during the day. But at night the moon shone so brightly that people found it hard to sleep.

"It means that most of the folk here are nuts," said Mr Tickle. He was humming a cheerful tune as he straightened the interior of the Snow-Beater which was now parked in a quiet street on the outskirts of the snow-covered town of Topsy-Turvy. The boys smelled the delicious scent of sausages frying on the hot stove in the Snow-Beater.

"Is it breakfast time?" asked Jack, definitely feeling hungry enough for more of Mr Tickle's wonderful fried sausages, but being utterly confused at what time of night it might be. Had morning come?

"Not exactly," replied Mr Tickle, "but since you two have travelled so far and must be in need of a snack, I thought we'd have a fry-up in the Beater before we settle for the rest of the night."

"Some snack!" said Timmy approvingly, looking at the sizzling sausages and bacon and eggs in the frying pan.

"I thought you'd like it!" said Mr Tickle, clearly delighted with their response.

"Are we staying in Topsy-Turvy?" asked Jack.

The two boys had taken it for granted that Mr Tickle knew what he was doing and that he was taking them wherever they ought to be. For the first time Jack had the faintest niggle that their confidence might be misplaced. And there was such an air of the simple and jovial about Mr Tickle that it was hard to imagine he knew much about anything beyond driving and cooking sausages.

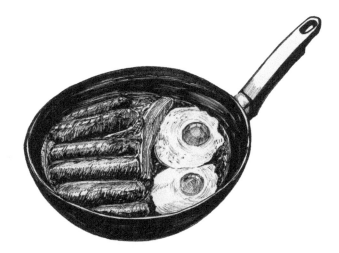

"Wellington and Sanity Stable have an apartment here for when they're working in Topsy-Turvy," explained Mr Tickle. "We can use it for the night. It's Bible-accessed so we can get in alright. Welly and Sanny are away just now. They're helping with the mission in Broken."

"Why can't we just stay in the Snow-Beater?" asked Jack, loath to leave the wonderful machine merely for someone's apartment.

"Well, now you mention it, perhaps we could," said Mr Tickle thoughtfully. "Of course, strictly speaking we shouldn't really stay on the streets of Topsy-Turvy, but all things considered, perhaps we'll be safe enough!"

The boys didn't know why they wouldn't be safe in this quiet place where the moon shone with such blinding brightness. It didn't feel dangerous.

"Do Mr and Mrs Stable tell the people here about the Lord Jesus?" asked Timmy.

"Of course they tell them about the Lord Jesus!" replied Mr Tickle. "There's nothing else worth telling folks about, is there?"

"I suppose not," conceded Timmy, taking a heaped plate from Mr Tickle and finding he was even hungrier than he had thought. Jack was pretty hungry too and they all tucked into their food, including Mr Tickle who ate with great enthusiasm whenever he could.

"Of course," explained Mr Tickle between mouthfuls of food, "Topsy-Turvy is a pretty hard place in which to reach people with the message of salvation through the Lord Jesus. They've got things so upside down and inside out here that it's hard to start teaching them about the message of the Bible and how they can be saved and put things right again!"

"What sorts of things do they have uh, upside down?" asked Timmy.

Mr Tickle shrugged as if the answer to that was actually pretty obvious. "You only need to look outside the window," he suggested.

For the first time, both Timmy and Jack carefully considered the view from the small, round windows of the Snow-Beater. They stared for a moment in utter disbelief at what they could see of the town of Topsy-Turvy. It looked like something from a completely alien world – in fact, from another planet entirely. The houses they could see were actually upside down, with their roofs on the ground and their foundations pointing to the sky. It was just as if the whole house had been turned upside down by a giant hand! There were a couple of trees in view and they were upside down too, with spindly, ugly roots towering above the ground, looking ashamed of being so displayed. All the plants and vegetables were also planted upside down, so Mr Tickle informed them, with all the greenery and flowers in the ground, and all the roots and dirty, ugly bits pointing to the sky.

"They still can't figure out why they don't grow fruit and vegetables successfully," said Mr Tickle, and off he went into a great gust of unrestrained laughter.

That made Timmy and Jack laugh too – because Mr Tickle's laughter was so infectious, and because the town was so incredibly, unbelievably, horribly strange and utterly ridiculous.

"Sometimes people put artificial plants on their roofs to try and look normal," said Mr Tickle, shaking his head, and then he got a fit of great, deep giggles again and was lost to sensible conversation for the time being. "I don't know why it always happens," he said at last, wiping the tears of laughter away from his eyes, "but every time I think about this town, it just makes me want to laugh! Of course, I also want to shake all the people upside down until they can see what an awful, silly mess they've made of everything!"

"But why don't they change things?" asked Jack, completely bewildered. Even the road sign he could see from the window was upside down; it wasn't very convenient to read the words.

"The people can't change things because they're so topsy-turvy themselves," Mr Tickle explained. "Their thinking, their way of living is so upside down and inside out that they can't change the town until they've sorted themselves out!"

Jack remembered the strange, but true, fact that the towns in Err took on the characteristics and nature of the people who lived there. So the towns and the people blended their natures until you looked out on the oddest, strangest places with the weirdest plants and weather and all sorts of things.

"Strictly speaking we're not meant to travel through Topsy-Turvy at night," confided Mr Tickle. "But I so wanted to see it all again, it's so very silly and so very funny…" he broke off, giving way to more prolonged laughter, at last wiping his eyes and continuing, "and I knew you would like to see it too! And if we leave very early in the morning, when the moon is sinking and everyone has gone to bed, then we should be fine! We can even spend the rest of the night parked at the Stables' apartment just to be extra sensible and sure!" He started up the Snow-Beater, reading directions from the Mission Detector for the Stables' apartment, and they began to move smoothly down the quiet street.

Timmy wondered why Mr Tickle felt the need to reassure them that they "should be fine." What hidden dangers lay in this strange place? Jack had a vague apprehension that Mr Tickle wasn't perhaps the most reliable tour guide, since he seemed to have the touching, but concerning, trait of putting amusement before safety and guidance. But the town beyond the windows of the moving Snow-Beater was calm and still, and there seemed to be no obvious trouble in this upside down place.

"What is upside down about the people?" asked Timmy, wishing he'd asked several more questions of Harold's longsuffering but very helpful Mission Detector and understood more about this exceedingly odd town.

Jack wondered about the people too. He had visions of folk walking around on their hands with their feet stuck straight in the air. But he didn't think it was a good idea to suggest this picture to Mr Tickle; Mr Tickle might never stop laughing.

"The people do everything the opposite to the way it should be," said Mr Tickle, and he seemed more serious now, as if the plight of the people of the town was no laughing matter compared to the ridiculous nature of the town of Topsy-Turvy itself. "So the children are in charge of everything, and the adults do what they're told! The children are really the ones that make the rules of the town. They run the Town Council and have their own Committees and such, and no one is allowed to touch them or say anything against them. I think they call it *self-expression* or *self-realisation* or some such thing, but whatever they call it, the kids run riot here and self-expression just means focussing on sin!"

Jack tried to imagine a town in which the kids made all of the decisions. It seemed like a great idea – and yet it was pretty scary too. Some kids weren't very nice; and if bullies ran the town it must be a horrible place to be.

"Consequently, Topsy-Turvy has the worst health, education, accidents, and incidents and family break-ups in this part of Err!" said Mr Tickle, and he definitely wasn't smiling now.

Jack and Timmy gazed out of the windows on either side of the Snow-Beater and tried to take it all in. There was a massive predominance of sweet shops and junk food available in the town centre which was, Mr Tickle informed them, because the children had banned healthy food and ate what they wanted. "I've heard that one advantage of their bad diet is that many of them are so fat that the Kid's Gangs can't easily chase you and beat you!" said Mr Tickle.

Timmy and Jack had absolutely no idea if Mr Tickle could possibly be serious or if this was a joke; but Mr Tickle didn't laugh.

Jack watched snow blow around them in strange, weird patterns. It was as if it was snowing – and yet it was not. "Does it snow uh… normally here?" he asked.

"Oh no!" said Mr Tickle with his more familiar chuckle, which sounded, however, somewhat restrained, "*nothing* is normal here. The snow doesn't fall down from the sky: it comes from all around, it might even come up from the ground! And then it blows around until it settles. That's why there isn't much snow on the ugly tree roots. It seems to just heap up in strange shapes around the streets!"

He was right. The more Jack and Timmy looked, the more strange even the mounds of snow looked in this place. There were several snowmen built in the streets too, all upside down and tumbling down with their heads on the ground. "The children have decreed that there's no school whenever it snows," said Mr Tickle. "Not that it makes much difference to them: they only go to school if they want to, and the school, Topsy-Turvy Progressive School, is all run by them anyway!"

Jack had a vague recollection of the time in Err when Timmy had come across boys from Topsy-Turvy Progressive School[1]. They had been big bullies of boys and he thought, as he glanced at Timmy's grim expression, that Timmy remembered it too.

But Jack quickly realised that wasn't the only reason for the grim expression on Timmy's face. And, for the first time since Jack had met him, the laughter vanished entirely from Mr Tickle.

"Trouble ahead," said Mr Tickle in a suddenly hushed and frightened tone. "Better put on your armour, boys."

CHAPTER 10
A DESPERATE ESCAPE

There was sudden silence in the Snow-Beater that seemed to last forever.

"Put on your armour, boys!" urged Mr Tickle.

Jack was about to remonstrate that they had no armour when Timmy gestured to a cupboard at the end of the Snow-Beater which was labelled 'Rescuer Equipment'. Mr Tickle was already wearing his armour and Jack noticed that his Bible was in a handy pouch just by his hand which was tightly clutching the steering wheel.

"What do they want?" faltered Jack, quickly slipping on his body armour and putting his helmet of salvation on his head, all the while looking through the front windscreen at the large group of big children, mostly teenagers, blocking the road some way ahead.

"I think it's the Snow-Beater they want," said Mr Tickle, and it wasn't reassuring to hear the panic in his usually cheerful tones. "Even though this isn't the best we have in the Rescuer fleet, it's still better than anything they're likely to have here! The kids on the Town Council don't like spending money on boring things like maintenance of public transport vehicles, even if they have abolished the lower driving age so any child can drive!"

"So they want to just…take it?" asked Jack.

"It's a town decree!" said Mr Tickle. "The kids of the town can decide what is theirs by right! Oh dear, oh dear! Whatever shall we do?"

"I'd like to see them try to take it from us!" said Timmy fiercely. "Can it gobble them up and turn them all into steam?"

Mr Tickle chuckled very faintly and Jack suddenly missed the warmth of his usual hearty chuckles. "Our best hope is to stay inside the vehicle and find a way around them," said Mr Tickle, his voice trembling. "If I could just get this Mission Detector to give us an alternative route to the Stables' house…But I think there's a problem with it!"

The problem might have been that Mr Tickle's fingers were shaking too badly to press the correct buttons, but Timmy was suddenly all action and quickly came to the rescue. He climbed into the front passenger seat beside Mr Tickle and, ignoring the on-board Mission Detector which was flashing '*Unknown Command*' in the most unhelpful manner, he quickly activated Harold's Mission Detector by pressing it and the small Bible together.

"It's Timmy here again," he said quickly to the screen.

"Hello, Timmy," the machine intoned.

Jack peered over the heads of Mr Tickle and Timmy at the group of kids blocking the road ahead. There seemed to be an assortment of frayed and scruffy uniforms amongst them, although what the uniforms meant he did not know. Some of them held big sticks as if they might be weapons and others were loading massive round snowballs into a couple of big catapult machines that looked as if they belonged to medieval days and should be displayed at an ancient castle. One of the snowballs was launched and smacked hard into the windscreen of the Snow-Beater with a big, sickening CRUNCH!

"They've got big rocks in the snowballs!" Jack cried in horror. They were now close enough to see the awful, frightening cruelty on the faces of the big youths. They looked savage and fierce and triumphant, as if they were glad to frighten the people in the Snow-Beater. For the first time Jack wondered what would happen to them if the children of the town stopped the Snow-Beater and got inside...

Timmy was very cool under pressure. He was not distracted by the massive snowballs with rocks inside them, not even when another crunched into the middle of the front windscreen and sent shattered glass flying around them. Timmy knew he mustn't let the small Mission Detector screen in his hand get distracted by confused commands and he asked clearly for the Detector to show the quickest route to Mr and Mrs Stable's house.

Another big snow-covered rock smashed onto the roof of the Snow-Beater and Jack retreated into the main compartment to look at the big dent that had appeared in the roof above the stove.

"Turn around, turn around," the Detector voice urged, as if it knew quite well what was happening.

Mr Tickle, who had little drops of sweat trickling down his face, swung the steering wheel violently and the big Snow-Beater skidded around in a circle even as another big rock smashed into a side window of the Beater and sent broken glass showering into the cabin.

The kids who had blocked the street now realised that the Snow-Beater was trying to avoid them, and Jack, who had been flung across the swerving Snow-Beater to the other side, heard their shouts of excitement and yells of pursuit.

"Take the next street on the left, called Kidsrule Street," the Detector said in its reassuringly calm, controlled, mechanical tones.

Mr Tickle, now silent and exceedingly pale, pressed his foot down on what appeared to be the accelerator and pulled the steering wheel hard to the left. The Snow-Beater obeyed the command and shot to the left, knocking over a streetlight (which Jack rightly assumed was only lit during the day), and completely destroying the upside down Kidsrule Street sign which Jack thought was a jolly good thing.

Another snow-covered rock, the biggest of them all, managed to reach the retreating Snow-Beater and smashed onto the roof. This time bright, cold moonlight appeared through the hole in the roof and the rock narrowly missed Jack's head and landed at his feet.

"At the end of the road, turn left," the Detector said, not in the least perturbed by the attack, and Mr Tickle, still standing hard on the accelerator, went roaring down the street and swung violently to the left. This time the Snow-Beater demolished a sign whose upside down words appeared to say 'Every Child has a Voice' (a statement which Jack thought was pretty obvious really), and then they were on a wider street down which the Snow-Beater roared furiously. Behind them kids yelled. On the side streets they flew past, children poured from homes, somehow alerted to the pursuit of the Snow-Beater. Ahead of them there were gangs of kids once more blocking the road.

"We'll have to leave the town!" Mr Tickle cried urgently. "It's not safe to stay!"

Jack considered that was something of an understatement. He had caught glimpses of some of the faces of the kids who were now all pursuing the charging Snow-Beater. They were cruel and intent on harm. How they had got to that fearful state he didn't know; but he did know that somehow they had to escape them.

"Quickest route out of Topsy-Turvy," said Timmy clearly to the Detector. He was white-faced himself but he managed to remain calm. "Urgent, please!" he added.

"Straight ahead!" responded the Detector immediately in what Jack was certain was an encouraging tone. "Suggest Snow-Blow action to clear road ahead!"

"The very thing!" cried Mr Tickle. "I don't know why I didn't think of it before!" He flicked a switch on the Snow-Beater, and, as they demolished two more streetlights, that were upside down and didn't do much good anyway since their light was so close to the ground, the Snow-Beater turned from gobbling snow for steam to blowing it out of the way. The kids in the road ahead dived for cover from the sudden onslaught of masses of fast-flying snow, and the Snow-Beater flew down the open road and straight out of the town.

Jack's last glimpse of Topsy-Turvy was another upside down sign which appeared to be the town's motto and proclaimed 'Freedom for Children is the Future! Please Visit Again.'

Jack couldn't think of any place he was less likely to ever want to see again.

CHAPTER 11
THE DAMAGED SNOW-BEATER

Mr Tickle kept his foot hard on the Snow-Beater accelerator until they were some miles from the town of Topsy-Turvy. He was somewhat slumped over the large steering wheel, which was really too big for his short, chubby arms. He looked faint and ill.

"The on-board Mission Detector warned me about going to Topsy-Turvy!" he moaned, all of the infectious laughter gone from his usually cheerful face. "I wanted to come and get you! It was an important mission! But it warned me…! And now whatever have I done? Whatever have I done?"

By that Jack assumed that Harold and Bourne had allowed Mr Tickle the special privilege of rescuing him and Timmy when they had been spotted praying in Err. He knew that Harold and Bourne could little afford to take time out to come after them, so Mr Tickle's offer, and the fact that it should have been a relatively straightforward mission, must have seemed like a good solution. And so it was – until now.

"I wanted to see how silly it all looked," said Mr Tickle forlornly. "Upside down things always make me laugh! But the horrible people! The awful children! I didn't know things were quite as bad as that! I thought we could get to the Stables' house without being seen!"

Even Jack wondered how Mr Tickle imagined they could have passed through the centre of the town of Topsy-Turvy, a town that was most awake at night, in a wonderful Snow-Beater that was far better than anything he had seen there, and not be noticed!

Thankfully Timmy, whom Jack considered had been something of a hero in the crisis they had just faced, took control. Suddenly Timmy seemed far more grown-up than Jack had known him to be before, and he was extremely thankful for his friend's presence in Err on this particular adventure. Mr Tickle was really too done-in to continue driving at speed, particularly as they entered a patch of woodland, and neither Jack nor Timmy thought the Snow-Beater would survive trying to gobble up a tree, especially after the various other wounds it had suffered in Topsy-Turvy – damage they had yet to assess.

"Nearest place to stop, please," said Timmy authoritatively to the small Mission Detector which seemed so much easier to use than the on-board Detector. The on-board Mission Detector still showed 'Unknown Command' and was flashing in a manner that was not reassuring. Timmy infinitely preferred using Harold's small machine that talked back to him.

"Topsy-Turvy is nearest town," the Detector announced, which, of course, they knew very well. But Jack wondered whether there was a note of disapproval when the mechanical voice mentioned the town of Topsy-Turvy, as if the machine knew they should not return there.

"The nearest place to stop on the road to Broken?" commanded Timmy, trying to assist Mr Tickle, who was looking increasingly ill, to steer the damaged, limping Snow-Beater through the trees.

"Avoid Topsy-Turvy," the machine agreed. "Nearest open services: twenty-two miles west, in the town of Broken."

"It's all my fault," said Mr Tickle. "I'm nearly retired but they'll stop me driving after this for sure!"

"Well, you can make pretty good sausages," Jack said feebly, trying to think of something to cheer up poor Mr Tickle.

"And my pension! What about my pension?" said Mr Tickle.

"I think we'll just stop somewhere near here," Timmy decided. Mr Tickle was still clutching the steering wheel somewhat wildly, as if he feared to let go. "Stop somewhere in the trees, Mr Tickle," Timmy said slowly and clearly. "And then we'll have a look at the damage to the Snow-Beater."

"Damage assessment on Snow-Beater?" the small Mission Detector asked politely.

"Can it really do that?" Jack asked, amazed at the small machine's capabilities. "I mean, it's not plugged in or anything! How can it even see what's wrong?"

Timmy shrugged. He was not inclined to question the Detector's capacity for genius; he was quite willing for it to do whatever it could.

"Damage assessment processing," the small screen announced reassuringly, and whilst it somehow remotely analysed the damage the Snow-Beater had suffered at the hands of the youth of Topsy-Turvy, Timmy managed to convince Mr Tickle to ease up completely on the accelerator and pull onto the side of the snow-covered road, beneath the trees.

"Oh dear, oh dear," said Mr Tickle. "You poor boys! Those dreadful children! How could they have attacked us like that?"

Timmy encouraged Mr Tickle to leave the driver's seat and take a more comfortable place in the back of the Snow-Beater. They brushed aside broken glass and snow that had come through the hole in the roof and the window, and Jack rummaged in the small kitchen area where there was a kettle and a cupboard with cups and plates and a few supplies. He thought he could just about manage to make a cup of tea for Mr Tickle; he had seen his mother do it plenty of times before. He wondered whether the Mission Detector, if it wasn't somehow assessing the damage to the Snow-Beater, could tell him exactly how to make a cup of tea. Nothing would have surprised him.

Timmy found a First-Aid kit in the Rescuer Equipment cupboard and both boys cleaned the cuts they had received from flying glass during the attack. Neither of them was badly hurt, and Mr Tickle didn't seem to have any wounds at all. Privately Jack was proud of the evidence of their war-wounds; both he and Timmy, with their scars and bruises, began to look like real Rescuers who had just escaped a dangerous attack.

Timmy walked around the inside of the Snow-Beater, looking grimly at the damage. There was a gaping hole in the roof above the wood-burning stove; half of the windscreen was shattered; and they knew there must be numerous dents and damage to the outside, and perhaps even to essential components of the Snow-Beater too. Timmy left the Snow-Beater to look at the outside damage and Jack managed to boil the kettle, find bags that looked like teabags, and added milk to the hot, murky liquid he managed to produce. Then he added plenty of sugar, which he had heard was good in emergencies (although he hadn't a clue why that might be), and carried the finished result carefully to Mr Tickle who was covered in a blanket on the soft, deep seat along the side of the Snow-Beater. It was quickly becoming cold in the Snow-Beater with the gaping hole in the roof; the fire in the wood-burning stove had gone out at some point during the chase.

Timmy re-entered the Snow-Beater. He didn't look very reassuring but he didn't say anything. He glanced at Mr Tickle who was looking utterly sad and forlorn and murmuring things about never being able to drive his beloved Rescuer vehicles again. Mr Tickle sipped the tea that Jack had made and didn't complain about the taste of it; Jack wondered if he even noticed what it was.

The small Mission Detector in Timmy's hand came alive again. "Damage report prepared," it announced, and Mr Tickle sat up a little straighter on the seat and looked anxiously at the boys.

"Damage to roof of Snow-Beater; requires immediate patching to make watertight."

"I think we knew that," murmured Timmy, looking at the gaping hole in the Snow-Beater roof through which the still-bright moonlight was streaming.

"Subsequent damage to stove and chimney; stove not fit for use."

Mr Tickle groaned and Jack looked in dismay at the top of the stove where the small chimney had been smashed by the rock. The whole wood-burning stove was now lifeless and there was only the slightest left-over warmth which was quickly vanishing through the open roof.

"Front windscreen requires replacing; driveable with care. Side panels dented. Broken window requires immediate patching to make watertight. Ability to snow-blow damaged; not recommended for further use. Flying ability broken and now disabled."

"It can fly too!" exclaimed Jack. "Why didn't we try that?"

"I don't have a licence to fly it," Mr Tickle said gloomily. "I've wanted to for years but I'm not recommended for training. You need a Capsule Licence to fly Rescuer vehicles."

Timmy hushed them, fearing to interrupt the Mission Detector that continued with its report. Jack thought he understood very well why Mr Tickle had not been recommended for flying machines as well as driving them.

"Half power on snow-beater driving mode." Mr Tickle groaned again but Jack thought it was pretty good that the Snow-Beater was able to go at all. Even if it only gobbled up half the quantity of snow that it had previously, they still might be able to make it to Broken.

"On-board Mission Detector malfunction," continued the small screen. "Use of on-board Mission Detector not recommended as not reliable. Damage to right runner; driveable with corrective steering."

There was a pause in which both Jack and Timmy held their breath as if there might be more bad news to come. Mr Tickle didn't seem to care; he sat with his head between his hands, murmuring apologies for their plight. But the invaluable Mission Detector had ended its report, and to Timmy and Jack at least that was good news. They could still drive!

Timmy sat down beside Mr Tickle. "I think we should be able to make it to Broken," he said. "We'll make you a bed so you can get some rest, and Jack and I will take it in turns to drive the rest of the way."

Mr Tickle was too tired and weary to protest. In fact, he was very grateful that Timmy was proving so capable. He watched as the boys found some plastic sheeting in the Rescuer Equipment cupboard and fastened it by various means over the gaping wounds in the Snow-Beater. Then they used the rest of it to screen off a small area at the front of the Snow-Beater. There was just enough room there for Timmy to sit in the driver's seat, Jack to sit in the front passenger seat, and Mr Tickle to lie on a heap of cushions and blankets across the floor just behind them. There wasn't much room to move, but they would be cosy enough, and at least being so close together would give them some warmth now they had lost the benefit of the wood-burning stove.

Timmy, appearing far more confident than he actually was, pressed a big button which said 'Start', and a jerky, uncertain hissing sound began. It wasn't like the fulsome hissing of the Snow-Beater of earlier, but it was something, and Timmy was profoundly grateful that anything at all had happened when he pressed the button. He had no idea how to drive the Snow-Beater, but Mr Tickle, now looking cosy on his cushion-laden bed on the floor behind the two boys, seemed perfectly content to leave them to the controls with absolutely no hint as to how any of them worked.

Timmy pulled a large lever which said 'Snow-Beater Mode' which he knew was the normal mode for driving the Snow-Beater and meant that it would gobble up snow and hopefully turn it into steam to propel them along. Then Timmy pressed the accelerator. He was as surprised as anyone when the big, broken vehicle left the shelter of the trees and moved slowly away. Perhaps he was the most surprised of the three: Mr Tickle appeared to have complete faith in him, Jack felt his friend could do just about anything, and only Timmy knew how frantically he prayed that they might manage the remainder of this long, strange, inexplicable journey and reach the town of Broken at last.

And so, slowly but surely, they started once more on the road to Broken.

CHAPTER 12
UNDER ATTACK!

As the lumbering Snow-Beater plunged valiantly through the deep snow on the road to Broken, the unnaturally bright moonlight gradually grew dimmer until the night slumbered quietly in darkness once more. It was a relief to know they were leaving the vicinity of Topsy-Turvy and that the things around them were the right way up again. Soon they could see the stars shining in patches of clear night sky between the dark, snow-filled clouds.

Sometime later, as they continued to move slowly and haltingly down the road, the sky began to lighten with the coming dawn and the long, distinctly odd, adventure-packed night drew to a close. They were all exhausted. Timmy did not sleep at all, even when Jack took the controls for a time. Mr Tickle drifted into a deep sleep – at least, that's what the boys assumed when deep, rumbling snores emanated from him – but as the sky grew lighter he awoke. Timmy was once more at the controls of the Snow-Beater. He had taken over from Jack when Jack's arms became tired from trying to keep the large, gobbling machine on a straight course, constantly correcting it from veering to the right because of the damaged runner. Not that Jack had complained. Even when it was damaged there was something wonderful about driving the Snow-Beater.

Mr Tickle was more alert after his sleep. He sat up on his cushioned bed, his white hair and beard sticking out all around him like a hairy kind of halo. As the Snow-Beater limped onwards he talked to the two boys about their experiences in the town of Topsy-Turvy.

"Why doesn't someone just take control of the town and sort it out?" asked Jack.

"It started as an experiment," said Mr Tickle. "It wasn't meant to be like that."

"An experiment about what?" asked Timmy.

Mr Tickle sighed. "I don't know all of the details of Topsy-Turvy," he said. "I really should have looked into it more carefully before I took you both there," he added, looking crestfallen all over again.

"But what was the town experimenting about?" prompted Timmy, fearing another prolonged outburst of remorse and despair from Mr Tickle.

"Well, it started with people thinking there was something good in everyone. They thought that people were good and that it's only the bad things around them that make people go wrong and do bad things. So the people who started Topsy-Turvy thought that if you put innocent children in a nice place, and give them everything they need, and let them do anything they want to do – then they will naturally do good things and the town will be a perfect place to live. That's how the children ended up in charge to start with."

It sounded like a reasonable idea: that there was good inside of everyone and that it just needed to be encouraged to all come out. "But it's not what the Bible says, is it?" said Jack.

Mr Tickle shook his head. "It certainly isn't," he replied. "The Bible says we're all ruined by sin; we're all wrong from the inside out[12]. So, if you leave even a child to their own devices, they will do wrong and sin."

"That's because Adam sinned[13], isn't it?" said Timmy.

"Yes," agreed Mr Tickle. "When Adam and Eve sinned, sin entered the whole world. And now sin is within all of us. We can't change or improve ourselves one little bit on our own. That's why we need the salvation God has provided through the Lord Jesus, Who was the only sinless, perfect Man Who ever lived. It's only through the death of the Lord Jesus that people can be saved from their sins and be made right with God[14]."

"So, over the years, Topsy-Turvy became like it is now?" asked Timmy.

"Yes," said Mr Tickle. "Although I didn't realise quite how bad it had become – otherwise I never would have dreamt of taking you poor boys through the town!"

"Never mind," said Jack kindly. "We didn't really mind." He looked helplessly at Timmy. It was hard to know how to comfort Mr Tickle; the boys had no idea how much trouble he would be in for taking them through the no-go town.

"I wonder how Topsy-Turvy became *so* bad though," mused Timmy.

"We should have thought to ask the Mission Detector more about it," remarked Jack.

They thought about the things they had seen in the town that had gone so badly wrong. Instead of bringing out good in people and proving that people didn't need God, the whole experiment just showed how bad people are inside, and how much they need help to be saved from their sins. Jack thought it was a bit like the way the Snow-Beater kept veering in the wrong direction: because it was damaged it couldn't drive straight anymore. When people were born into the world they were already damaged by sin – and so they always went towards sin and wrong.

"The human heart is desperately wicked,[12]" said Mr Tickle sadly. "Really the Topsy-Turvy experiment is the opposite to what the Bible says about everyone in the world being a sinner[15] and the Lord Jesus being the only way[16] to be saved. All Topsy-Turvy proves is that when people are left to their own devices they go deeper and deeper into sin. Until you have something as awful as that…that horrible, horrible town and those dreadful, dreadful children!" He shuddered at the memory of their fleeting time in the town of Topsy-Turvy.

"I don't think the town can last much longer the way it's going," remarked Timmy. "It's like a war zone already!"

Mr Tickle nodded solemnly. "And it will only get worse unless people put things right the way God planned," he said.

For, without the solution God offered to the problem of sin, Topsy-Turvy would always be upside down; disgraced and ruined beyond repair.

Dawn had broken across the sky and Mr Tickle fell asleep again, content to leave his fate in the youthful hands of Timmy and Jack. Timmy continued to drive and Jack tried to stay awake and talk to him. He gave Timmy pieces of the Christmas cake from his rucksack which was the only food within easy reach. They were both cold and cramped and hungry but neither of them commented on those things. There wasn't any point in complaining when there was nothing they could do to improve their situation, except keep driving towards the nearest town, Broken, where they hoped their friends could help them.

They didn't see another soul or another vehicle travelling through the snowy landscape. Jack thought he saw a herd of deer on the edge of a forest once, but it was hard to tell through the splintered glass of the windscreen, and after that fleeting sign of life there was nothing else. There was just the snowy road, the occasional snowy patch of trees or forest, infrequently a snow-covered sign, and sometimes the road twisted and turned slightly between raised banks and small hills.

At some point in the journey the terrain changed, and now they were in a rocky, rolling landscape, still snow-covered, but strangely desolate. It was daylight, although there was no sun because thick, dark snow-clouds obscured the morning sky. The trees they saw were snapped and broken, and the odd signs they saw were also broken and unreadable. They entered a stretch of thicker woodland where the road twisted and turned in a strange fashion around fragmented and distorted trees whose branches and limbs seemed mostly strewn on the ground. The snow was less deep under the shelter of the trees and the Snow-Beater moved more quickly until…

CRUNCH!

CRASH!

WHAM!!

Mr Tickle would have leapt right out of his blankets but he got entangled somewhere in the process and wriggled helplessly, trying to get free.

Jack almost jumped out of his seat and Timmy's knuckles were white as he clutched the steering wheel and tried to control the violently lurching Snow-Beater.

"What was *that?*" gasped Jack.

"Jumping grasshoppers!" exclaimed Mr Tickle, muffled by the blankets he was still trying to remove from his head.

"Grasshoppers?!" exclaimed Jack. "I really don't think it could be…!"

"I think that was just an expression," said Timmy. "I don't think it's actually grasshoppers." He sounded grim, as if he knew what it really was.

There was the sickening sound of glass smashing as something hit the side of the Snow-Beater and yet another window was broken.

And then, through the gaping wounds of the poor Snow-Beater came voices that all three of them knew and that Timmy had already guessed somehow lay behind the attack.

"Ooh, pour broked Beater-Beater!" mocked a cold, shrill voice.

"But how could they throw such big rocks?" cried Jack. "Meddlers are only tiny…!"

"Teeny r wee?" said a Meddler.

"Teeny-weenys broked yoor big Beater-Beater!"

Mr Tickle at last emerged from his blanket, his white hair wild from being so entangled. It appeared that the Meddlers had had some hand in thus entangling him and they laughed – gleeful, horrible, shrill laughter as at last Mr Tickle got free. He did look pretty funny and it seemed that the Meddlers thought so too. They stopped throwing big rocks – although it still was not clear how they had managed that – and invaded the Snow-Beater through the thin plastic sheeting that Jack and Timmy had used to cover the holes the Beater acquired during the attack in Topsy-Turvy. There was no stopping the Meddlers. They were too small and slippery to catch, and now they were simply everywhere.

They descended on poor Mr Tickle and pulled his ears, his hair and his beard. They pulled the stuffing from his cushions and the buttons off his shirt. They got into Timmy's rucksack and pulled the Christmas cake to pieces, throwing crumbs around as if they were at a children's party. They got into the small kitchen cupboards and broke the cups and plates. And their horrible, shrieking voices mocked and scorned the old man who had brought the boys to this snowy wasteland in a Snow-Beater which now, thanks to the Meddlers' attack, could go no further.

The Snow-Beater was completely broken.

Their journey had come to an end.

CHAPTER 13
THE CALL FOR HELP

The Meddlers had no mercy on the occupants of the stranded Snow-Beater.

"Stop!" cried Jack. He swiped wildly at the air which was thick with the small flying imps who seemed different to the Meddlers he had fleetingly glimpsed before. These Meddlers wore small, red jackets and they were utterly formidable in their multitudes. Jack hit several of the creatures but that only brought him their unwanted attention. And it was clear that their main target was poor Mr Tickle.

"It's because I've been despairing," cried Mr Tickle. "The Red-Jacket Meddlers torment Christians who give way to doubts and despair and self-pity!"

"Get out!" shouted Timmy, angry with the awful Meddlers who tormented the old man with accusations and taunts.

"Oldy mannie fayled!"

"Oldy mannie all gone wrongey!"

"My Bible," gasped Mr Tickle. "The answer is in the Bible!"

Jack didn't know where Mr Tickle's Bible was. If his Bible had been near him then it was probably torn to shreds by now. The air was so full of bits of broken and torn things and swarming Meddlers that it was impossible to tell what damage they had done. Jack thrust the small Bible he had found in Harold's jacket pocket into Mr Tickle's hand.

"You can accuse me of no wrong that God cannot forgive," shouted Mr Tickle, clutching the Bible which seemed to calm him and make him strong. "The blood of Jesus Christ cleanses from all sin![17]"

They all heard the hisses and boos of the small, silly creatures in tiny knitted red jackets; these creatures who preyed on people's worst fears about themselves and meddled until they were in utter despair. They were nothing in themselves, these Meddlers. They were tiny, and puny, and weak. But when they appeared in numbers they became an awful, terrifying enemy.

"God's strength is made perfect in weakness![18]" cried Mr Tickle, quoting from the Bible.

There was definite dismay amongst the hoards of tiny vicious creatures who accused him so mercilessly. They seemed to pause in the havoc they were wreaking.

"Know use Fickle-Tickle!" said a sulky, far more uncertain-sounding Meddler.

"I know that in me nothing good dwells,[19]" cried Mr Tickle, once more quoting from the Bible. "Of course I'm no use! None of us is any use at all apart from the goodness and grace of God!"

It was astonishing to see the effect this had on the Meddlers. There had been so many of them that they had seemed innumerable. But as Mr Tickle attacked them with the sword of the Spirit, the Word of God[4], they fell away from him and fled through the holes in the sides and roof of the Snow-Beater as if they were too terrified to stay. Not one single Meddler remained and for a moment the three inhabitants of the wrecked Snow-Beater stared at each other in silence.

"Wow," Jack said at last. "That was amazing, Mr Tickle!"

"That, my boy," said Mr Tickle, sounding quite solemn and perfectly calm, "that was the greatness of the Word of God, the Bible! Living and powerful![20]"

"The Meddlers certainly don't like the Bible much," said Timmy.

Suddenly Mr Tickle laughed, and the two boys who were watching him – rumpled, with white hair sticking out in every direction, his clothes torn, and with bits of Timmy's mum's Christmas cake sprinkled all over him – were so relieved that they laughed with him.

They were stuck in the middle of nowhere, surrounded by snow, with no more food, in a battered Snow-Beater that could go no further. There was no point in a Damage Assessment this time. Everything around them was broken beyond repair. Their laughter died away and they took stock of their smashed surroundings. They were very cold and very hungry and very tired. They started to pick up the main broken bits in the Snow-Beater and once more patched up the gaping holes. They had to secure shelter somehow, even if they had nothing else.

In the quiet stillness of their broken surroundings, there was suddenly a strange sound that didn't belong in the forlorn patch of woodland around them.

"Did you hear that?" asked Jack.

"I thought I heard something," admitted Timmy.

"M-Meddlers?" asked Mr Tickle with a tremor in his voice.

"I don't think so," said Timmy.

But both he and Jack knew by now that Meddlers were very clever at imitating people and making things seem other than they were. They heard the sound again. Very faint; so distant they could almost ignore it as a trick of their imagination.

"H-help! H-h-help!"

Timmy looked at Jack.

Jack looked at Timmy.

On no account did either of them want to leave the shelter of the Snow-Beater – such as it was – and venture into the woodland. Even if the Meddlers had fled, that wouldn't stop another attack, or something worse from an even more formidable creature.

"What shall we do?" asked Jack.

"I-I think we'll have to go and see," said Timmy. "It might be that someone really needs help somewhere out there."

"You must each take a Bible," said Mr Tickle briskly. "Don't forget the power of the Word of God, will you? We've just proved the Bible can defeat any enemy! Don't make my mistakes and forget the power and goodness of God!" Mr Tickle was more than willing to go on the expedition, but they all realised that Timmy and Jack would make much quicker progress on their own. "I'll stay and see what I can find in our emergency supplies and carry on tidying up!" said the old man cheerfully. "We might even start a fire to keep warm!"

They took Timmy's rucksack – which was still in one piece – with them, and both Timmy and Jack tucked a Bible in their pockets. Once again, very feebly, they heard the cry. "H-h-help! H-help!"

And they set out into the wood, trying to find the way.

"Who would have thought," said Jack, after they had walked for some time in silence, "who would have thought that we would spend Christmas week like this?!"

"Are you still glad to be here?" asked Timmy.

Jack looked around the strange, misshapen, broken trees that looked hideous and monstrous in their fractured, ugly shapes. They were walking through deep snow, working hard to make a track; feeble sunshine was trying to break through the dark, forbidding clouds of another threatening snowstorm. "I'll be glad afterwards," said Jack, and Timmy laughed.

They heard the cry for help several times on their trek and followed the sound. But nothing else disturbed the morning calm. Now and again they spied the spindly, wicked faces of Meddlers hidden in the ruined branches of the trees. Now and again they heard their muttering and accusing. And once, they heard them chanting a very silly rhyme:

"Fretters for the Old,

Distractions for the Young,

Issues for the In-Betweens,

Our Plan have we begun!"

"That's a very bad poem," said Jack.

"Just ignore them," said Timmy. They had gained a victory over the Meddlers, but they were not anxious to suffer another attack.

But the Meddlers, although clearly discontented, stayed crouched and sulking in the trees.

Suddenly Timmy stopped and pointed ahead. In a clearing in the smashed trees, slumped by a large swamp-like pond, was a girl. It didn't seem at all likely that it was really and truly a girl, out here in the middle of nowhere, lying senseless by an icy, dirty pond. But it certainly appeared to be the case.

"Is she…is she *dead*?" Jack asked in awe.

"I don't think so," said Timmy. "She was calling for help, remember?"

"Unless she's just died," said Jack solemnly.

"Hey!" shouted Timmy, walking forward hesitantly. "Hey there! Are you alright?"

Somewhat to Jack's surprise, the motionless, slumped figure raised her head and stared at the two boys.

"Have you come to rescue me?" she asked. Her voice was feeble and hoarse-sounding; as if she had very nearly lost it altogether.

"I suppose we have," said Timmy.

"I was…I was praying for help," said the girl.

Jack followed Timmy towards the girl. He was very glad Timmy was leading the way. Where a girl fitted into their strange adventure he wasn't sure. He wondered whether he would rather deal with things like Meddlers than a girl who had clearly been crying.

"You were calling for help," said Timmy. He reached the girl and crouched down beside her.

"Was I?" she murmured, sounding surprised.

"We heard you," Jack said helpfully. He noticed the girl was about Timmy's age, with tangled gingery hair. He didn't really know what she looked like – except that she was a mess. She had obviously been crying for a long time because her face was red and blotchy and patchy. She was wearing a warm jacket, which was just as well, but all her clothes looked very dirty and wet and she looked extremely cold.

"Can you, uh, can you walk, do you think?" asked Timmy.

"I expect so," said the girl. "Who are you?"

"I'm Timmy," said Timmy, "and this is Jack."

Jack thought the girl looked surprised. "I think I've heard about you," she murmured.

Jack thought she had probably lost her mind too. It was very unlikely this bedraggled apparition had heard of them.

"I'm Josie," said the girl.

"How did you…uh, where did you come from?" asked Timmy.

"I ran away from Broken," said Josie.

"Oh," said Timmy.

"That's where we were supposed to be going," said Jack.

"To help the Christmas mission?" asked Josie.

"Yes."

The girl sighed. "I want to go back there too," she said.

"Well," said Jack, "you can come with us." He was glad to contribute something positive in this most confusing situation, and then he remembered they couldn't get there either. "At least, you can come with us to the Snow-Beater," he added, "but it's broken, I'm afraid."

Josie didn't seem to care much about that. "Everything is broken," she said, and her voice caught on a sob. Jack was very much afraid she was going to start crying again and he was glad that Timmy was proving so capable. "Do you see in the pond?" asked Josie. "Do *you* see *you* are broken? I'm broken in pieces! All in pieces!"

Jack decided she had definitely lost her mind. How were they supposed to deal with a mad, crying girl? But then he remembered what they had prayed about early on their journey. They had prayed for people who were lost, that they might be rescued too. Perhaps Josie, strange and inexplicable though it might be, was the answer to that prayer.

Timmy was looking into the pond where Josie was pointing. It wasn't a very nice pond. It had weeds and rocks poking through the icy surface, and underneath it looked muddy and polluted. It was all frozen on the top, but there wasn't much snow on it. And when you looked through the ice…

"Jack!" said Timmy. "Look into the pond! What do you see?"

Jack looked down into the cloudy ice. He couldn't see his reflection at all; not one little bit of it. "I see…" he looked more closely. "I see, yes, I think I see the shadow of a…cross," he said slowly.

"That's exactly what I see!" said Timmy.

The girl Josie gave a wail of anguish. "You don't see what I see?!" she asked wildly. "You don't see yourself all smashed and broken? Look at me!"

They peered over her shoulders and looked with horror into the pond. Jack shuddered and hoped that Josie didn't notice. For, in her reflection there wasn't the simple shadow of a cross. Josie's reflection was Josie.

And she was smashed and broken beyond repair.

CHAPTER 14
THE MENDING OF JOSIE

Neither Jack nor Timmy could think of words to comfort Josie. It was undeniable that the murky, icy, swamp-like pond showed her to be dreadfully broken, with cracks all over her and pieces missing, just like a ghastly, horrific jigsaw puzzle.

"Uh, perhaps you shouldn't look," said Jack, which was the only immediate solution he could think of. At least when Josie wasn't looking into the water she didn't look quite like *that*.

"I think we should go," said Timmy, trying to be firm. "We'll get back to the Snow-Beater and talk to Mr Tickle."

Josie didn't ask who Mr Tickle was. Either she knew or she just didn't care. Jack didn't think he would care about much else if he looked as broken as Josie. Why was she all broken like that when he and Timmy only reflected the cross?

"Just like the people in the town," cried Josie, sobbing. "Just like the people in Broken! Just like poor Melody!"

"Who's Melody?" Jack murmured to Timmy.

"It doesn't matter right now," said Timmy. "The important thing is to get back to shelter. Then we'll see what should be done."

"Right," said Jack.

"Nothing like the River Self," Josie murmured as they tentatively and rather awkwardly helped her to her feet. "That was a nice reflection."

"Uh, right," said Timmy, anxious only to be on their way.

It took a moment for Josie to regain the feeling in her legs and feet, but once they began walking she managed quite well on her own. It was slow going, but at least they didn't need to search for the way. The trail they had broken through the snow was clear and they could easily follow it back to the Snow-Beater.

Josie didn't complain. She trudged on between Timmy and Jack, now and again murmuring something about being broken and wanting mending, apparently unheeding of the discomfort of being bedraggled, and wet, and cold.

They were some way into the twisted trees when they heard the muttering of the Meddlers.

"Ooh, silly boo-hoo girly!" said a shrill, unwelcome voice.

"Girly-girl all broketed!"

"Know mendy-mendy for boo-hoo girly!"

"Shut up!" said Timmy sternly. "Leave her alone!"

"They were at me for hours," said Josie wearily.

"They're the Red-Jacket Meddlers," said Jack. "Mr Tickle said they were the Meddlers of doubt and despair."

"Well, they're good at their job then," said Josie. "They have convinced me that I'm broken beyond mending!"

"All broketed!" said a Meddler's voice. "Poor girly-girl know mendy-mendy!"

Jack saw the tiny Meddler hop across a branch in the tree. You could spot these Meddlers by their bright red jackets: tiny splashes of colour through the distorted trees. The Meddlers' beady eyes were trained on poor Josie, who walked through the snow with her head hung low.

"Shut up!" said Timmy again. "And anyway, you're liars, every one of you!"

"Yew a liar, yew a liar..." chanted the Meddlers.

"It's not true that Josie can't be mended," said Timmy. "And you know it too! The Lord Jesus can mend anybody!"

There was instant stillness in the trees around them. Jack wondered if the Meddlers had fled but he glimpsed them still sitting in the branches, their small, scrawny hands and fists held tightly over their ears to block out Timmy's voice and the terror of his message. Their faces were scowling, bitter and cruel; but they were defeated.

At last they were in sight of the poor, battered Snow-Beater.

"What happened?" asked Josie, rousing herself at the sight.

"It's a long story," said Timmy. "But the last straw was an attack by the Meddlers."

Josie seemed unsurprised that Meddlers could have reduced the grandeur of the wonderful Rescuer Snow-Beater to such a sad state. She had clearly had a hard time at the hands of the Meddlers. "Broken," she whispered, "everything broken!"

Jack was pleased to see that Mr Tickle had started a fire in the clearing outside of the Snow-Beater. "There's plenty of broken wood anyway!" the old man said cheerfully. "That's one good thing about so much being broken! Well, and who do we have here?" He greeted Josie and, far from being surprised they had reappeared with a strange, clearly damaged girl, he immediately took control of the situation. "You come right by the fire, my dear," he said. "See, here? That's right. A lovely log to sit on! We'll get you dried out and warmed up in no time!" He asked no awkward questions. He seemed to know exactly what to do. "I even found some cookies in the emergency supplies," he confided. "So we'll not only be warm, we won't starve either!"

"Is-is someone coming to rescue you?" asked Josie, her teeth beginning to chatter from the cold.

Mr Tickle took her damp jacket and draped a couple of blankets around her shoulders. "Well, now," he said comfortably, "well, now, that's a very good question, isn't it?"

"We can't raise help," said Timmy.

"We've been praying for help," said Mr Tickle.

"Don't you have a Mission Detector?" asked Josie.

"The batteries have run out," said Jack. At last the small, indomitable Mission Detector lay silent and unresponsive, flashing one last message: '*No battery for further exchange*'. And none of them had been able to figure out how to recharge the Mission Detector in such shattered surroundings.

"Can I see?" asked Josie. She looked astonished at the small Mission Detector that Timmy placed in her hand. "But that's Harold's Detector!" she exclaimed. "He's very proud of it!"

"Right," said Jack.

"Do you know Harold?" asked Timmy.

"He's my cousin," Josie said briefly. She was looking at the small screen. She didn't ask how they had got Harold's Detector; she seemed to be figuring out how to use it. "Most of the latest gadgets are powered by light, or heat," she murmured. She wrapped it in the edge of her blanket and pushed it towards the fire. "That might do it," she said. "Better leave it for a bit."

Mr Tickle gave them all cookies to eat and they sat around the fire. It was past lunchtime, but they all knew it was no good thinking about food; apart from the cookies, there was none. No one asked Josie exactly why she had been in the middle of a wood so many miles from Broken; Jack and Timmy thought Mr Tickle was the one to deal with that particular puzzle. In the meantime Josie was quiet, looking into the crackling flames, with an expression of despair.

"Do you really think it's true that I can be mended?" Josie asked at last. She was thinking of what Timmy had said to the Meddlers.

"Uh, yes, I do," said Timmy. "I was thinking about that verse you used against the Meddlers, Mr Tickle," he added. "The one about the blood of the Lord Jesus cleansing us from *all* sin[17]. Does that mean He mends all the broken bits and makes you completely whole again?"

"In fact, it's better than that," said Mr Tickle, nodding vigorously. "The Lord Jesus doesn't just mend you, He makes you a new person: completely brand-new! That's why the Bible says we need to be *born again*[21]. I'm afraid there's nothing that can be salvaged or improved in us, instead each one of us needs to be made a new person altogether!"

"I thought I could improve myself," said Josie. "But I know now I'm just horribly broken!"

"That's what our sinful nature[12] has done to us," said Mr Tickle. "We're born with it, and unless we ask the Lord Jesus to save us, we're just what you said: horribly, horribly broken! There's nothing good inside us at all!"

"I thought there were at least some good bits," said Josie. "I thought plenty of people were good and happy without the Bible."

"There are no good bits at all," said Mr Tickle. "The Bible says that no one is right before God[22]. We all need the Lord Jesus to be our Saviour."

"I suppose it's a bit like the people of Topsy-Turvy," said Timmy. "They assumed there was something good in everyone. But if people are rotten and wrong all the way through, then there is nothing that can be improved!"

"Exactly, Timmy!" exclaimed Mr Tickle. "And when people start to realise that, they stop trying to improve themselves and instead trust what the Lord Jesus has done."

"It's truly as simple as that?" asked Josie. "We just ask the Lord Jesus to save us and we're mended and whole?"

"It's really as simple as that," assured Mr Tickle. "The Lord Jesus has already done enough to deal with all the sins in the world when

He died on the cross[23]. All you need to do is ask Him to save you, and the price He paid for *your* sins is put to *your* account! Then you'll be completely new. No cracks, no broken bits left at all!"

They didn't hear what Josie said when she prayed to God to save her. She was crying again and Jack and Timmy left Mr Tickle to comfort her. When they returned Josie was smiling as they had not imagined she could.

"It's alright now," she said. "I'm mended! Brand-new inside out!" And she laughed with joy. "I know it's a bit of a nuisance," she said when they were all once more gathered around the fire. "But I'd quite like to go back to the pond in the wood. I want to look and make sure I'm not…not broken anymore, you see? I want to see the cross instead of brokenness, like Jack and Timmy did."

Timmy and Jack once more accompanied Josie on the trek through the trees, following their old trail. Somehow the walk didn't seem as far this time and there was not a Meddler in sight. Very soon they were back at the banks of the ugly, murky pond, and, with only a slight hesitation, Josie looked deep into the glassy surface.

Timmy and Jack looked with her. No longer was her reflection cracked and smashed and broken.

Instead there was the cross.

CHAPTER 15
RESCUED

Mr Tickle had not been idle while the others revisited the pond. He had gathered more firewood and rigged up a large covering that stretched between the Snow-Beater and the fire. None of them wanted to be gloomy about their prospects, especially when Josie was so happy, but all of them wondered what would happen now, and if and when help might come. And Jack in particular was extremely hungry.

"We should have caught Meddlers and cooked them over the fire," said Jack.

Josie giggled. "I wish they could have heard that," she said.

"I'm not sure there's a lot of meat on them," remarked Timmy. "And I bet they would be bitter or poisonous inside!"

"Oh, look!" said Josie suddenly. She had removed the Mission Detector from its place in the blanket by the fire and held it in her hand. The screen blinked as if it was waking from sleep. The battery indicator was green and unwavering. "Now," said Josie, "now we can call the Control Room and get help!"

"The Control Room!" exclaimed Mr Tickle. "That's it! I knew there was something else I should have remembered! In an emergency, always call the Control Room!"

Josie handed the Mission Detector back to Timmy. "It knows your voice," she said. "You'd better tell it to connect with the Control Room."

"Uh, alright," said Timmy. "Control Room, please," he said to the small screen in his hand.

"Connecting, Timmy," intoned the machine.

Josie giggled. "I always wanted one of these," she said. "Although it used to be because I wanted to learn all about Err!"

Jack thought he would quite like one too. He wondered what Dad and Mum would say if he asked them for a Mission Detector for Christmas!

There was a crackling sound coming from the Mission Detector, and then, "Come in, Harold, uh, I mean, Private Wallop! How can I help...?" They were warm, friendly, and surprisingly youthful tones, and Jack immediately recognised the voice.

"Dusty!" exclaimed Jack.

"Dusty!" exclaimed Josie, jumping off her log by the fire. "Dusty! It's Josie!"

"Josie?" said the voice of Dusty Addle. "Well, I never! I thought you were lost! The Rescuers from Broken are out searching for you! Or...are you with Harold there? This is his Detector I'm receiving..."

"Oh," said Josie. "I thought the Rescuers might not bother to search for me since I've caused so much trouble for them all. And, no, Harold's not here. We've got his Detector and now we all need help!"

"Right," said Dusty briskly, suddenly all business-like. "Details can wait. Go ahead with your request, please."

"Uh, do you know our exact location, I mean, can you see where we are on a map or anything?" asked Timmy.

"Just coming clear…right about now!" said Dusty cheerfully. "Your signal is now showing clearly and I'm looking right at you! You're only a dot, so I can't see what's wrong or anything, but you're in Fracture Wood, approximately eight miles east of Broken."

"Wow," murmured Jack, trying to imagine what Dusty was looking at. Jack had never seen the marvellous complex machines and the massive Central Mission Detector which recorded all the movements of all the Rescuer vehicles, and of Rescuers themselves, in the land of Err.

"Well," said Timmy. "We're completely broken. Our Snow-Beater was attacked, and now…"

"Not Snow-Beater Welly by any chance?" interrupted Dusty. "I lost a Detector signal from Snow-Beater Welly some time ago!"

"Yes, poor Snow-Beater Welly," murmured Mr Tickle with a sigh, "and all my fault!" But he smiled when Josie went and slipped her hand through his arm.

"But you rescued *me*!" she said comfortingly. "It's just as well you broke down when you did!"

"How many are in your party?" asked Dusty.

"Uh, there are four of us now," said Timmy.

"I'm here too, Dusty," said Jack.

"Well!" exclaimed Dusty. "There's clearly a story behind this uh, transportation incident! I thought you were safely in Broken, Jack, since the Rescuer Transporter has definitely arrived there!"

"It's a long story," said Jack.

"I look forward to hearing it!" said Dusty. "But I'd better stick to business. You would like Rescuer assistance?"

"Yes, please," said Timmy. "Is that possible...?"

"Anything is possible," said Dusty brightly. "Rescuers will be with you as soon as I can raise them. I expect they'll come from Broken. That's their nearest location. You might have to sit tight for a while longer though, there were several breakages last night and there has been a recent snowstorm which has caused the usual wreckage!"

"That's OK, thanks very much," said Timmy, glad that any help was coming at all and not inclined to question the strange reference to snow causing wreckage.

"No problem!" said Dusty. "Safe onward journey!" He said it confidently, as if their troubles were already over. "And uh, Jack?

Thanks again for the blanket! It looks great in my room!"

"Oh, that's OK," said Jack.

"Over and out!" said Dusty, and the screen flickered quietly to blankness once more.

"Help is on the way," said Timmy.

"It's as simple as that!" said Jack.

"Just like that," said Mr Tickle contentedly. "And all thanks to this young lady here!" and he patted Josie's hand.

Once the call with Dusty ended, Josie and Mr Tickle explained something about the Central Control Room located deep in the Academy of Soldiers-of-the-Cross. From Josie's description the Control Room seemed to be able to see and do everything they could possibly have needed on their entire broken journey. The boys didn't reproach Mr Tickle for not mentioning this very helpful and relevant service earlier – they accepted his shamefaced explanation that he 'thought he could do everything himself' and, as Josie once more reminded the old man, it was as well they had come the way they had, and broken down when they did, because she was rescued and mended! It was the one thing that did not fail to cheer up Mr Tickle. Josie's rescue, and subsequent salvation, certainly put their broken journey in a whole different light.

Snow began to fall again. Mr Tickle, Timmy and Jack took it in turns feeding the fire with wood to keep it going. They took all the blankets and any cushions that weren't burst and ruined, and brought them to the shelter Mr Tickle had made. Josie lay down under some blankets and, while the wind began to blow more fiercely, and snow began to cover the floor of their inadequate refuge, Josie slept the sound sleep of a deep, lasting peace. Mr Tickle, Timmy and Jack huddled under the covering too. They were cold, cramped, and hungry. How much longer could they last without being rescued? Eventually exhaustion overtook them, and one by one they fell asleep.

Jack was awakened by a strange sound. He was looking at the rumpled hair of Timmy, who was next to him, still sleeping deeply. He moved cautiously so he didn't disturb him, and saw Mr Tickle on his other side, also fast asleep, his white hair looking wilder than ever, his expression peaceful and content. He was snoring, but that wasn't what had woken Jack. Close by was Josie, sitting up amongst her blankets, looking around. It was dim daylight in Fracture Wood. Jack had no idea what time it was: for all he knew they could have slept for a whole week and missed Christmas entirely.

He didn't feel particularly alarmed at the alien noise that was approaching them from somewhere beyond the trees. His tired mind felt curiously unafraid, and he gradually recalled the details of their long night journey, how they had come to be in a deserted wood somewhere between the towns of Topsy-Turvy and Broken, and how they had rescued Josie.

"Did you hear the noise too?" whispered Josie.

Jack nodded. He wriggled away from the two sleepers and put on his boots. Josie collected her blankets and put them over still-sleeping Mr Tickle whose nose was blue with cold. Then she followed Jack. The sun was low in the sky, peeping from between clouds and making bright sparkles on the snow. It was nearly the end of the day and Jack judged it was probably still the same day in which they had rescued Josie. How many other strange things could be packed into such a short space of time?

He looked around him, wondering what it was that had made the strange whirring sound he had heard. He didn't think it could have been Meddlers, but his hand clutched his Bible, just in case.

Josie and Jack walked through the fresh, deep snow that had fallen while they had all been sleeping. The unusual whirring sound had stopped.

"It might be someone coming to rescue us," said Jack hopefully. He wondered what sort of rescue contraption could possibly make that strange whirring sound.

"I almost feel like running away again," said Josie with a sigh.

"I don't think you should do that," said Jack.

"No," agreed Josie. "But I've been thinking about seeing them all again, after all the trouble I caused. My brother, Bourne…well, I don't know what he'll say!"

"I met Bourne, and Harold," said Jack.

"Did you?" asked Josie, clearly amazed.

"I travelled with them in the Rescuer Transporter, with Mr Tickle too," said Jack.

"Well," said Josie, "I bet you haven't caused them as much trouble as I have. And Hugo and Henry too, and Henry has been so patient with me even though I expect she wanted to strangle me most of the time!"

Jack wasn't sure how he had earned the privilege of being comforter or adviser to Josie. What was he supposed to say? He was pretty sure it would all be alright in the end, and besides…

"Well, if the angels in heaven rejoice when someone gets saved[24]," he said, "then I'm sure all the others will be happy about you being mended."

"I've heard of that!" said Josie. "I've heard lots of things from the Bible, but I just didn't believe them. Imagine angels in heaven rejoicing over someone like me!"

"Uh, exactly," said Jack. "So, I expect Bourne and Harold, Hugo and Henry and all the others will just be happy that you're a Christian now."

The Red-Jacket Meddlers seemed to have gone from the trees and there were no malicious stirrings in Fracture Wood.

"Hey!" cried a voice from somewhere ahead. "Anybody there?"

The voice was distant and slightly distorted. For a moment Jack wondered whether it was a trick of the Meddlers. He looked through bent trees and branches. He wanted to ask the same question. Who was out there?

"Over here!" he yelled at the top of his voice, and then he wondered if he had been wise. After all, he had no idea who this was. Josie clutched his arm. She, at least, seemed to think he knew what he was doing.

Muffled footsteps approached them through the snow.

And then, at the first sight of two men, Josie was off at a run. She stumbled through deep, fresh snow, over fallen tree limbs, plunging straight towards the newcomers. "I'm mended!" she cried joyfully. "I'm all put right! The Lord Jesus has healed me!" And she ran straight into the welcoming arms of her brother, Bourne Faithful.

Harold Wallop had come with Bourne to rescue them, and Jack led him back to the Snow-Beater which sat battered and torn and smashed in a patch of sunshine.

Harold was horrified at the damage to the Snow-Beater but neither he nor Bourne, when he arrived with Josie, said anything to Mr Tickle. Instead Bourne shook the old man by the hand and thanked him for rescuing his sister. Mr Tickle was waking up rather slowly from his cold, muddled sleep and took some convincing that the rescue party of Harold and Bourne was actually real and that the whole thing wasn't a dream.

"You're welcome, sirs," he kept saying. "You're very welcome…" And he cast nervous glances at the wreckage of the Snow-Beater as if he knew there was yet to be a reckoning.

There was very little worth saving from the Snow-Beater so it didn't take them long to collect their few belongings. They all walked through the fresh snow and the broken trees, and left the poor, battered Snow-Beater for a rescue team to salvage another day. Harold helped Mr Tickle who, despite being cheerful, was very tired and shaky after their ordeal.

And very soon, before them, Jack saw the most extraordinary sight through the trees.

CHAPTER 16
THE MENDING CENTRE

Jack thought he had seen just about every strange and wonderful mode of transport there could possibly be in the land of Err. But when he saw the Rescue Capsule in a clearing in Fracture Wood he wondered if this might just be the most incredible thing he had yet seen. The Rescue Capsule was round and it had windows facing in all directions. Just now it stood on long legs, sticking out from the snow and appearing strangely alien – but it was also secure and clean and neat and tidy amidst the broken trees and scattered limbs and branches around it.

"It's one of the smaller models," said Harold. "Just a six-seater."

Jack didn't think the number of seats was likely to be the most interesting feature of this machine that actually looked like a flying saucer!

"Sorry we took so long to get to you," said Bourne. "There was another snowstorm in Broken which always takes some time to clear. In the end we had to use a Capsule to get to you because all the roads around Broken are still blocked with heaps of snow. Snow-Beaters get damaged because there are too many rocks and broken things hidden in the snow around the town. It messes up their snow gobbling ability and breaks all their insides when they swallow a rock!"

"Actually, even if there isn't snow, the Capsule is just about the best thing to travel in around here," said Harold. "All of the roads are broken up or in really bad repair. *Everything* is broken here!"

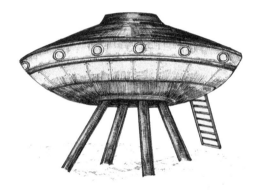

As they skimmed over trees and fields on their way to the town of Broken, Jack and Timmy realised the truth of Harold's words about *everything* being broken. Snow covered the land and crowned the buildings and plants and trees and everything else they could see, but even the pretty white blanket couldn't disguise the fact that the town they approached was in a very bad state of repair indeed. The roofs of the houses were patched, or wonky, or tumbling down; some houses were missing windows; some were missing chimneys, and smoke billowed from big holes in the roofs as the people inside tried to keep warm. The evening was approaching and darkness was falling when they hovered over the town. Jack saw feeble pinpricks of light from lampposts that were all at odd angles, some even lying on the ground, trying to shine despite their sad, broken state. The trees were twisted, stunted, distorted, and falling over. They even saw a few Christmas trees, and these were also broken. Some of the lights on the trees weren't working and one of them had toppled over and was half buried in snow. There were several big yards containing broken Atobs and household appliances and other paraphernalia, which basically looked like massive rubbish dumps. They could hardly believe it when Harold informed them that these dumps were repair yards where people tried to patch up and mend their broken things so they could use them again…until they broke once more.

"It's the main occupation in the town," said Harold, "mending broken things!"

"Well, they're not very good at it," Jack remarked bluntly.

"Or the people work in one of the many bandage factories in the town," said Josie.

"Bandage factories!" exclaimed Timmy.

Josie nodded. "One of the main trades of the town seems to be making bandages and sticking plasters to sell to the people," she said.

Jack tried – and failed – to imagine what people did with all the bandages churned out by the bandage factories. Were they going to a place where people were all falling apart?

"Just about all of the shops sell bandages and sticking plasters and things that are useful to patch or mend or repair," said Harold.

"It's not a very exciting place to do your Christmas shopping!" commented Josie.

"That's a good one!" chuckled Mr Tickle. "Imagine bandages for presents for Christmas Day! Ha, ha!"

"I despised the people of Broken," said Josie. "I thought I was nothing like them. But if I hadn't found the Lord Jesus, I would have been wearing bandages too!"

Soon the Capsule hovered over a large building in the centre of the town which was extraordinarily different from the rest. Standing tall and proud, in the middle of the rubble and ruin of the town of Broken, the Mending Centre looked like a castle from a fairytale. It shone with light and strength; it was comfortable and majestic; snow covered the turrets and roofs; the whole stronghold was sturdy and unbroken.

"The Mending Centre belongs to the Rescuers and other Christian workers," Harold explained as Bourne pushed buttons and twisted levers and the round Capsule began to descend smoothly towards the vast castle. "We're all staying here. It's used in missions and outreach, and judges sometimes use it too when they visit to assist with law enforcement. It's the only maintained and completely weatherproof building in town."

The long legs of the Capsule were extended and it came to rest gently on the ground. Harold opened the door and lowered the steps. One by one they descended.

At last they had arrived in the town of Broken.

The details of their arrival in Broken – the warm, delicious supper which was the first good food they had eaten in what felt like years; meeting their friends again, Hugo and Henrietta Wallop, and Jack's own particular friend, Hezekiah Wallop; the rejoicing about Josie becoming a Christian; this vast, ancient castle in which they had slept – they all felt fuzzy and unreal when Jack awoke the following morning. He was lying in an enormous bed which had a post at each corner and was hung with curtains and coverings of rich colours and patterns. Jack parted the hangings and saw Timmy sitting up in another bed across the room, looking around as if he, too, was trying to remember how they came to be in this ancient, fairytale castle.

Light filtered through the thick curtains at the windows and a strange thumping sound came from somewhere outside. Timmy got out of bed and went to the window. He gave an exclamation of amazement and Jack immediately leapt out of bed and joined him. It was snowing the most massive snowflakes they had ever seen. Actually, it wasn't possible that they were snowflakes at all. It was just as if the sky was throwing big round snowballs to the ground below, which thumped down upon the broken town, causing even more damage to patched roofs and tumbling chimneys. The great white chunks broke apart when they hit the houses and ground, spreading shapeless lumps of snow all around.

"I think this explains why the snow isn't smooth and normal here," said Timmy. "Remember when we flew over the town yesterday? It was all bumpy, not smooth snow at all!"

"I remember Mr Tickle saying that the snow in Broken was, well, broken," said Jack. "Snowflakes can be maimed and ruined, or it can snow snowballs like this!"

"I expect all the weather here is broken," said Timmy.

"And snow like this just makes everything even more broken," said Jack. He was glued to the window, looking out on the poor, tumbledown town which was getting battered by ferocious snow. "No wonder they need this big castle to keep them from being bashed to pieces!" he said.

They had learned the previous evening that something called a Rescuer Enquiry was to take place that day, and Jack and Timmy and Josie were all going to be a part of it.

"What exactly did Harold say the Enquiry was about?" asked Jack, as he finished buttoning his now clean and dry shirt, not taking the time to wonder how it had been transformed.

"I think it's just a discussion about exactly what happened on our journey," said Timmy.

"Do you think Mr Tickle will be in trouble?" asked Jack, as they left their room.

"I don't know," said Timmy. Both of them hoped that Mr Tickle would not be in any serious trouble for taking them into Topsy-Turvy and everything that subsequently happened. But it was hard to see how he would not be at least partly blamed for their disastrous journey. Except…

"Perhaps they'll let him off when they hear the bit about rescuing Josie," said Jack hopefully. "That must count in his favour!"

"I think they're trying to discover whether there was some mechanical or other failure that led us to Topsy-Turvy," said Timmy.

Jack considered how the truth might appear to a panel of important Rescuers: that Mr Tickle took them through Topsy-Turvy because the town made him laugh. It wouldn't look particularly positive for the old man. He only hoped he wouldn't lose his job.

Timmy was confidently following a passageway through the castle which had a tartan carpet in blues and greys. All the floors of the Mending Centre were thickly carpeted to save endless breakages when the broken people who worked there dropped things. The tartan patterns on the carpets showed which part of the building you were in, and there were small tartan swatches on the walls which showed you where you ought to go. Timmy led the way unerringly to the big dining hall, assisted by the lovely smell of bacon and sausages.

Breakfast was already in progress, and the large hall, which was set out with long wooden tables and benches, was already full of chattering people. Jack spied Mr Tickle who raised his hand and waved. He was sitting with a tall, stern-looking man who was Mr Wellington Stable. He had the appearance of a very capable, forbiddingly sober military man about him and Jack thought he might even be able to manage the out-of-control kids in the town of Topsy-Turvy.

Mr Wellington Stable finished his breakfast and vacated his place at the table.

"I believe I'll see you two boys soon," said Mr Stable, "with Mr Tickle here, at the Rescuer Enquiry this morning."

"Uh, yes, sir," said Timmy.

Mr Tickle smiled bravely at the two boys and then leaned forward confidentially. "But never mind about that," he said. "What did you think of the snowstorm here this morning, eh? Snowing snowballs!" He began to chuckle. "It always makes me laugh," he said, wiping funny tears from his twinkly eyes. "I didn't dare laugh in front of Welly Stable, of course, especially since I've just broken his Snow-Beater!"

"I can see how that might be awkward," said Timmy drily.

Jack nearly choked on an inadvertent giggle.

"But he's been very good about it," said Mr Tickle, "very generous indeed! A real Christian gentleman!" He eyed his nearly empty plate, with one solitary sausage in the middle of it. "I only ate four sausages this morning," he said. "I haven't much appetite before this Enquiry. I hope it doesn't take as long as the last one!"

"Have you, uh, have you been to a Rescuer Enquiry before, then?" asked Jack, watching Mr Tickle spread strawberry jam on his remaining sausage.

"Oh yes," said Mr Tickle. "I've had my fair share of Rescuer Enquiries in the course of my long career." He sighed. "It's strange the things that can go wrong on rescue missions," he said. "So many things to remember! So many things can go wrong!"

Jack imagined there were plenty of things that could go wrong with Mr Tickle in charge of Rescuer equipment. But he hoped for the old man's sake they wouldn't be too hard on him. He could imagine how upset Mr Tickle would be if he couldn't drive his beloved transport vehicles anymore.

A lady approached the table to take their orders for breakfast. It was very hard not to stare at her. Apart from the fact that she looked a bit like the dinner lady in Jack's school – which was really nothing remarkable – she wore bandages on one arm, one hand, and, most bizarre of all, wrapped around a part of her apron. The bandaged lady, whose name was Gladys, brought Jack and Timmy plates full of cooked sausages, and bacon, and fried eggs. There was plenty of toast and milk and tea too. Jack noticed that the plates and cups were plastic and he wondered if Gladys had broken all the china ones or if they just didn't use them here. Perhaps they were all broken. He was very intrigued with her bandages.

"Is she hurt?" he asked when Gladys had left.

"People in Broken always wear bandages," said Mr Tickle.

"That certainly explains the bandage factories," murmured Timmy.

"I don't think the bandages will do that lady much good on the outside of her clothes," observed Jack.

"No," agreed Mr Tickle, "but that's not really the point."

"Isn't it?" said Jack.

"People wear bandages because they feel broken inside, don't they?" said Timmy.

"That's exactly right, Timmy!" said Mr Tickle approvingly. "They've got so used to wearing bandages over and on any imagined broken bits that they hardly know they do it anymore!"

Jack thought about Josie's broken appearance and how much she had seemed to need bandages when they first saw her by the pond. But all the same, it was very strange. "Do the bandages really make people feel better?" he asked.

"The people of Broken cover up their problems with sticking plasters and bandages, but these things don't really help them at all," said Mr Tickle. "People feel they are covering up the problem of their brokenness so that no one can see it anymore. So it makes them feel better about it. But of course, it doesn't really deal with it at all!"

"Why doesn't someone tell them?" asked Jack.

"I think that's exactly what the Rescuers here *are* doing!" said Mr Tickle.

"Oh," said Jack. "You mean the Christmas mission..."

"The message of the Lord Jesus Christ and how He came into the world to save lost people[25] from the power of sin and the awful brokenness that sin brings, *that* is the only thing that can *really* heal the people of Broken," said Mr Tickle.

When Mr Tickle left the two boys to finish their breakfast they were joined by the twins Hugo and Henrietta Wallop, and their younger brother Hezekiah – or Zek – Wallop, who was Jack's particular friend. Mr Tickle had left them rather solemnly. "I'm going to prepare," he said seriously as he departed. "I need to put on my thinking cap so I don't get muddled. I must make sure I tell the exact truth at the Rescuer Enquiry. Only the truth will do!"

"I wonder if there's anything *we* should do to prepare for the Rescuer Enquiry," said Jack.

"I shouldn't think so," said Hugo. "They would have told you if there was."

"You don't actually *know* that, Hugo," said Henrietta.

"It's actually common sense, Henry," returned Hugo.

"I don't think you've got the only common sense around here, Hugo," said Henrietta.

"Girls and common sense…" began Hugo.

"We want to hear all about your journey!" said Hezekiah. "Harold wouldn't let you talk about it last night!"

"And then he didn't tell us anything when you'd gone to bed!" said Henrietta, also eager to know the details.

"Harold says the details are covered by Rescuers' confidentiality," remarked Hugo.

"Which is just an excuse!" said Henrietta.

"Here's your spy watch, Jack," said Hezekiah. "The twins said I could look after it when you left it in Aletheia the last time you were here![26]" He removed the watch from his wrist and reluctantly handed it to Jack.

"That's alright, Zek," Jack said generously, "you can wear it until I go home again."

Hezekiah happily returned the watch to his wrist again. "So, tell us all about your journey here," he said. "It must have been amazing if there's a Rescuer Enquiry about it!"

"Did Mr Tickle really take you right through the middle of Topsy-

Turvy?" asked Hugo. "That's what everyone is saying, but they're not sure how it happened. Perhaps the on-board Mission Detector took you the wrong way. It's possible it malfunctioned. These things can happen you know…"

"You don't really know that, Hugo," said Henrietta.

"Well, I didn't say that's actually what happened," said Hugo, "I was only saying…"

"But did it really happen?" asked Hezekiah. "You going through Topsy-Turvy?"

"Yes," said Jack.

"Haven't any of you been there?" asked Timmy.

"It's a no-go area," said Hugo. "No one goes there unless they've got specific prayer cover and a lot of specialist equipment!"

"That explains quite a lot," said Timmy drily.

Henrietta giggled. "Was it really bad?" she asked, her eyes aglow.

"Pretty bad," admitted Timmy.

"It was only because of Timmy that we got out of the town at all!" said Jack.

"I don't think it was me at all," said Timmy.

"It was," said Jack earnestly. "Mr Tickle sort of…well, panicked," he added, and then wondered whether that was disloyal.

"And I can't believe you rescued Josie too!" said Henrietta. "I still can't believe she's mended and is now a Christian! That's the most amazing thing of all! She's so different to how she was before. You really wouldn't believe what she was like…"

"Remember what Harold said, Henry," said Hugo.

"I keep forgetting," said Henrietta. "But I mean to remember. Harold told us that because all Josie's sins have been blotted out and taken away, and God remembers them no more, then we shouldn't remember them either![27]"

"We'd really like to come to the Rescuer Enquiry and hear all the details," said Hezekiah.

"But Harold has said *absolutely not!*" added Henrietta. She gave a very good imitation of her eldest brother and the others laughed.

"We've found a hole, though," said Hezekiah in an excited whisper.

"It's not exactly hard to find holes in Broken," said Hugo.

Henrietta giggled.

"Anyway, we can see the Enquiry Room through the hole…" said Hezekiah, and then trailed off, for their much-admired cousin, Lieutenant Bourne Faithful, wearing a smart uniform and clearly on business, arrived at the table to collect Jack and Timmy for the Rescuer Enquiry.

"I hope I didn't give us away," said Hezekiah in a troubled voice as Jack and Timmy followed Bourne away. "I'd hate them to block up the hole!"

"Never mind, Zek," said Henrietta. "I'm sure Bourne didn't hear you."

"I suppose," Bourne observed as he led Jack and Timmy down yet another tartan passageway into a part of the castle they had not explored. "I suppose Zek and the others think they are the first to discover the hole in the wall of the Enquiry Room."

Jack and Timmy exchanged glances. Did this tall, scarred warrior know all about what his cousins planned? And his eyes were twinkling too, as if he were only amused at the thought of them eavesdropping on proceedings. Bourne smiled somewhat whimsically. "I think Harold and I thought we were the first to discover that hole when we were younger too!" he said.

Then they stopped before a large door with a bold sign on it.

It simply said, 'Enquiry Room'.

CHAPTER 17
THE RESCUER ENQUIRY

There were five people already present in the Enquiry Room when Jack and Timmy entered with Bourne. It was a large room with mellow wooden panelling and big, gilt-edged paintings of important-looking people on the walls. The carpet was a warm red tartan. On the far side of the room, by a big window, there were eight chairs set around a massive table, three on one side with their backs to the large window, and five on the other side facing the window.

In two of the chairs with their backs to the window, facing Jack and Timmy as they entered the room, were Wellington and Sanity Stable, the Outpost Rescuers for the towns of Broken and Topsy-Turvy and others in the region.

Facing Mr and Mrs Stable across the table was Harold Wallop, and sitting beside him was Mr Tickle on one side and Josie Faithful on the other. Jack couldn't help thinking how incongruous small, round Mr Tickle looked in the smart, stately surroundings of the Enquiry Room. He seemed to have shrunk – or maybe the surroundings and the lofty ceiling made him look even smaller and less significant than before. Mr Tickle was wearing a borrowed suit that was too big for him, and, more startlingly, had a red cap perched on his head. Jack wondered whether this was Mr Tickle's thinking cap. He had said he was going to put it on: was it possible there were real thinking caps in the land of Err? The red cap at least subdued some of Mr Tickle's white hair, but he had forgotten to comb his beard. It was sticking out all over the place, and a stray ray of sunshine that was shining through the window made it once again appear like a very hairy, upside down halo.

Josie looked remarkably different. She was clean and tidy and her ginger hair was brushed and gleaming. She looked pretty. She was certainly nothing like the figure of abject despair that the boys had stumbled across in the forest clearing. She grinned at Jack and Timmy as they took their seats, but she was fidgeting nervously with her hands. She would, after all, have to tell her story about running away. Bourne took the seat by Mr and Mrs Stable on the other side of the table. And so they were all assembled.

Jack was glad that, from his seat, he had a great view of the street beyond the big window and the wall that surrounded the Mending Centre. He could see right into the town of Broken. It had stopped snowing big snowballs and there were a few folk venturing into the street. The snow lay in odd, roughly-shaped heaps where the snowballs had smashed haphazardly into things and disintegrated into misshaped chunks. The people in the street had to climb around and over the heaps, and there were already a few trails made by the passersby. Jack could see two women walking slowly through the snow with shopping bags over their arms. One had a woolly hat with a white bandage around it. The bandage was coming undone in the stiff breeze that was blowing down the street. It really looked very silly and he could not understand how people thought that such ineffective fixes could heal or hide their brokenness. It hardly even covered it up for a day.

Bourne, as the Lieutenant responsible for coordinating the Christmas missions, was in charge of the hearing. Jack stopped looking at the lady in the street with the white bandage waving like a flag from her woolly hat, and began to pay attention to the Enquiry.

"There's nothing to be worried about," Bourne was saying. "We just want to get to the bottom of what happened on your journey here, update our records with any new information, and see what we need to learn from...uh, various incidents." Mr Tickle sighed deeply at Bourne's statement. The crinkly laugh lines around his eyes hadn't quite disappeared, but he looked rather anxious. Jack wasn't all that surprised that Mr Tickle was concerned. He had the feeling that Bourne, and certainly Mr Wellington Stable, might not readily understand the 'various incidents' – particularly since the debacle in the town of Topsy-Turvy really stemmed from Mr Tickle's love of, and amusement at, upside down things. Jack did not think that Mr Stable shared a love of upside down things at all.

"Mrs Sanity Stable will take notes," Bourne gestured to Sanny Stable who acknowledged this by lifting the small stick she was using to make notes on a Mission Detector screen. She made soft tap-tapping sounds as she made a note of something on the screen. Jack wished it was a talking Mission Detector that told them what she was writing.

"How do you wish me to log the record of this Enquiry, Lieutenant?" Mrs Stable asked in a most efficient tone.

"I think, since the bulk of the account is likely to involve the town of Topsy-Turvy, we'd better log it under Topsy-Turvy Updates, and also under uh…Rescuer Transport Incident."

Mr Tickle sighed deeply again. He was thinking about the smashed Snow-Beater which would be towed to the Transport Workshop in Aletheia for evaluation and, if possible, repairs. Yes, it was certainly a noteworthy 'Rescuer Transport Incident'.

"Now, we'll commence with…" began Bourne.

"Excuse me, Lieutenant," Sanny Stable said politely, "but I'm not sure of the full names of Timmy, Jack and Josie. I need an accurate record. And also, Mr Tickle's full name would be…?"

Harold coughed. Jack thought it sounded suspiciously like a laugh.

"Of course," agreed Bourne evenly.

"My name?" faltered Mr Tickle. "Yes. Thank you, dear lady. Thank you so much. Gamrie Tiberius Tickle, at your service, ma'am."

Harold coughed again and grabbed hastily for a cup and the water jug from the centre of the table.

Jack looked curiously at Mr Tickle, thinking he might be telling a joke and waiting for his rumbling laughter to confirm this. But Mr Tickle was sat straight in his chair, for once as serious as a judge.

"The spelling of Tiberius, would it be with an 'a' or a 'u'?" Sanny Stable asked earnestly.

Mr Tickle looked pleased at the attention, but perplexed at the question. "It starts with a 'T', dear lady," he returned with equal earnestness.

Harold seemed to produce a peculiar sneeze and frantically grabbed for his hanky. Timmy also seemed beset by a fit of coughing and Josie stifled a laugh. Jack pictured Hugo and Henrietta and Hezekiah looking through a hole at them all, listening to every word and enjoying the unexpected amusement at the Enquiry.

Bourne was riffling through the papers he had in front of him, his head bowed low.

Mr Stable was frowning. "Really, Sanny," he said. "I'm sure we don't need…"

"Now, now, Welly," returned Mrs Stable calmly. "You'll be the first to complain if we don't get all the details correct!"

"On this occasion I don't think we need to worry about full names," said Bourne, looking up with an expressionless face. "There is only one Mr Tickle on our fleet of Rescuer Transport drivers and he will be, uh, easily recognised in our databases. A first initial is quite adequate, thank you, Mrs Stable."

"Well, if you're sure," she said doubtfully, and she dutifully tapped the screen with her stick.

"We really must get on with the details of the incident," said Mr Stable.

"Right," said Bourne. "We'll start our discussion from the time we first noticed Jack was missing from the Transporter on the night of the 20th of December. That part of the incident should be straightforward enough."

"That's the same day I…ran away," murmured Josie.

"Shall I record the year?" asked Mrs Stable, her stick poised above the screen.

"Really, Sanny!" protested Mr Stable. "We must get on with the discussion!"

Mrs Stable calmly recorded something on the screen, not in the least perturbed by her husband.

"I was the first to notice Jack was missing!" said Mr Tickle, looking pleased at having something positive to contribute. "I was the first, remember?"

"Yes," said Bourne. "Go ahead with as many details as you can."

"We were in the vicinity of the Health and Healing Hamlet," said Mr Tickle. "I particularly remember that, because I thought Jack might want to look out for the square apple tree they've persuaded to grow there. It's the funniest thing…" and suddenly, for the first time in what seemed like far too long, Mr Tickle gave way to great gusts of helpless, rumbling laughter. He was clearly trying to contain himself, but Josie got the giggles too, and Jack and Timmy and Harold were laughing at Mr Tickle, and for a while Sanny Stable had nothing whatever to write on the screen. "Oh dear, oh dear," said Mr Tickle, wiping the tears of laughter away from his eyes. "Square apples! It always strikes me as so funny! Whatever will they think of next?"

"Are there really square apples in the Health and Healing Hamlet?" asked Josie.

"There are stranger things than that there," murmured Harold.

"This is off the point," said Bourne firmly.

"Come now! Come now!" contributed Mr Stable, spearing the now quietly chuckling Mr Tickle with a most serious glance.

"I knew you would like to see the square apple tree," Mr Tickle said to Jack, not catching Mr Stable's sober look.

"They surely don't grow apples in the winter!" said Mrs Stable, her writing stick still poised above the screen.

"Oh no!" said Mr Tickle. "But you can see the tree from the road, and it just looks so funny, even without apples! It's all so square, you see!"

"Here we go again!" murmured Harold.

Mr Tickle tried to restrain his laughter, but it had clearly been building up for too long and just needed to all come tumbling out. He had not been able to truly laugh after the incident in Topsy-Turvy, and now it was as if all of his laughter had been bottled up and shaken very hard and someone had just popped the top off the bottle.

"So, Mr Tickle, you went to check on Jack, to see if he wanted to see the uh, square apple tree…" prompted Bourne.

"I carefully put the Transporter on auto-mode for just a minute," said Mr Tickle, clearly emphasising the fact that he had been *careful* on that occasion at least. "And I went to see if Jack was still awake. And that's when I realised that he wasn't in the Transporter at all! You remember that?" Mr Tickle looked anxiously between Harold and Bourne.

"Yes," said Bourne. "We stopped the Transporter and decided we would locate the nearest Rescuer Snow-Beater transport to send after Jack, and Timmy of course, although we didn't know about Timmy at that point."

"Our Snow-Beater was the nearest one. It was parked at Drink-n-Drugs-Upon-Hollow," said Mr Stable. "And so you dropped Mr Tickle off at the Snow-Beater shelter in Drink-n-Drugs and continued your journey to Broken in the Transporter, while Mr Tickle was…uh, despatched after Timmy and Jack."

"And a very great honour it was too!" said Mr Tickle. "A very great honour, sirs!"

"Yes, well," said Mr Stable, and cleared his throat.

"The next part of the incident is obviously the bit we know the least about," said Bourne. "Timmy and Jack, perhaps you can tell us how you met up and a little about your journey to the point at which Mr Tickle discovered you."

"A very great honour it was, too," murmured Mr Tickle. "A very great honour to discover them!"

The details of Timmy's entry into Err and Jack's discovery of him in Plod's shelter on Apathy Road did not make a great deal of sense to Welly and Sanny Stable, or to Bourne. Josie listened with avid attention, clearly enjoying the account, and Harold, who knew all about Timmy's and Jack's previous adventure in the land of Err, was more accepting of the strange details. But Sanity Stable was sitting with her stick poised above the Detector screen, not tapping in any words at all.

"Most interesting," she murmured as they gave their account. "Really, that is *most* interesting! Are you sure you don't want these details recorded, Lieutenant?"

"I don't see what use they would be to us," said Bourne. "I mean, of course they're interesting," he added. "But I don't think there's much we can learn from them."

"No," Welly Stable agreed firmly. "I think we'd better leave them unrecorded." He looked with astonishment at Timmy and Jack. He seemed unable to decide whether to believe, or disbelieve, their story. He had never heard anything like it before. Mr and Mrs Stable were the most sane, steady, and unimaginative people. That was partly why they had been chosen for Outpost Rescuer work amongst various challenging towns such as Topsy-Turvy and Broken and Drink-n-Drugs-Upon-Hollow and even the awful town of Mindless: because they were least likely to be affected by the error and afflictions and mind-illnesses of the townsfolk in these places.

"I really feel as if I could write a book about this!" exclaimed Sanny, as Jack and Timmy finished the account of their adventure at Plod's scruffy shack.

"Really, Sanny," murmured Welly in incredulous reproach. "I never thought you could be so fanciful!"

"Oh, I dare say I wouldn't be able to make it believable enough," admitted Sanny. "But someone really ought to write a book about this!"

"Dear me, Sanny," Welly murmured again.

"Anyway," Bourne intervened, "let's cover the rest of the boys' journey to the point at which they met up with Mr Tickle."

The Rescuer Enquiry Panel found this the far more believable part of their tale, although Jack considered that it would be the part that no one at home would believe. But Meddlers, and a moon that shone as brightly as the sun, and the small, clever Mission Detector were all things that the Stables and Bourne and Harold could understand.

"I'm sorry I lost the note from your pocket," Jack said to Harold when they explained how the Meddlers had tormented them and grabbed everything they could.

"What note?" asked Harold.

"There was a note in your pocket," said Jack. "I didn't read it, but the Meddlers were sort of reading it and it was…" he trailed off in sudden silence when Timmy nudged him sharply. Jack had been about to say *a love letter*.

Bourne smiled slightly as if he knew quite well what Jack had been about to reveal. "Well, I don't think the details of the note are important for this Enquiry," he conceded. "But perhaps Harold and I could chat with you about that afterwards."

Harold coughed and glared at his cousin.

"And I saw Jack and Timmy on my Mission Detector screen when they prayed to be found!" said Mr Tickle, anxious to tell the creditable part of the tale. "And then we were off together in the Snow-Beater to…" he paused, realising where his story would end. "To Topsy-Turvy," he concluded, and there was a deep, sad sigh from Mr Tickle.

"When was the decision taken to go into the town of Topsy-Turvy?" asked Bourne.

"It was all my fault," said Mr Tickle. "It was my decision. The dear boys didn't know anything of it, they went to sleep and I just drove there."

"We're not seeking to blame anyone, Mr Tickle," said Mr Stable. "We want to know the details to see if there's anything else we should learn or do as a consequence of the incident."

Perhaps Mr Tickle feared that the 'anything else we should do as a consequence of the incident' might be the bit where he lost his beloved Rescuer Transport driver responsibilities. He gave another heartfelt sigh.

"Were you aware of the Mission Detector's warning about the town of Topsy-Turvy?" asked Bourne.

"I just thought I could manage," said Mr Tickle dolefully.

"Why exactly did you *particularly* want to go that way, Mr Tickle?" asked Harold.

"It's the town," explained Mr Tickle. "It's so topsy-turvy! It just makes me laugh! It's the thought of everything so upside down and inside out and the wrong way around! It's just so funny!" And, not particularly helping his case, but quite helpless to do otherwise, Mr Tickle began to giggle: prolonged giggles, the type that are impossible to keep in and infectiously funny when they come out, exactly like the giggles that come when you're tickled. "Oh dear, oh dear," he gasped helplessly between gusts of laughter. "Houses on their roofs! Foundations at the top! Doors in the sky! Streetlights on the ground! Tree roots in the air! Oh dear! Oh dear!...I'm so sorry, sirs..." He began to regain control of himself.

"It is a bit funny," said Jack, trying to stick up for Mr Tickle. "I even thought the people might go around walking on their heads!" Jack had hoped to help Mr Tickle's rather hopeless case; he had not intended to precipitate another fit of helpless laughter from Mr Tickle. But he certainly did just that.

"Ha Ha!" laughed Mr Tickle. "Hee Hee! I never thought of that!

People on their heads! Feet and legs waving at the sky! Everything upside down! Ha Ha!"

Jack looked with consternation at Mr and Mrs Stable and Bourne across the table. He certainly didn't think he had done Mr Tickle any favours by making him laugh again. Just as he supposed, Mr and Mrs Stable didn't look as if they'd ever found upside down things as amusing as Mr Tickle clearly did, and Bourne was fidgeting with bits of paper again, as if he wished the whole Enquiry would come to an end.

"I think we should move on from the decision Mr Tickle made to go to the town of Topsy-Turvy," said Bourne. "I don't think there's anything, uh, that we can learn from that, uh, aspect of things."

"Quite," said Mr Stable tightly. "Perhaps we could discuss some of the things that happened there."

It wasn't all plain sailing, but the details gradually emerged. They described their predicament, and then their escape from the town of Topsy-Turvy, with the awful youths of the town assailing and assaulting them on every side. Mrs Stable wrote quickly and frequently during that account, her stick making constant tap-tapping sounds on the screen.

"The town sounds worse than ever," remarked Bourne.

"I think it can sometimes be worse at Christmastime," said Mr Stable. "The Yellow-Jacket Meddlers of Strife invade the town and try to un-do any good we do telling people about the peace that the Lord Jesus came to bring. The Meddlers love the strife they can so easily cause amongst the youth of the town. It's where they usually go for their annual Christmas party!"

Jack tried – and failed – to imagine the mayhem of the Meddlers' Christmas party in the town of Topsy-Turvy.

"I don't think we need to discuss the Meddlers' Christmas party, Welly," said Mrs Stable, pausing in her tapping of the Mission Detector screen. "It really is a most disagreeable occasion!"

"Do the Meddlers have the party, uh…up-up-upside down?" asked Mr Tickle. He could hardly complete his question for the giggles that began once more to break over the Enquiry.

Bourne shuffled his papers. "I think we'll have a break for tea," he said.

CHAPTER 18
THE PLAN OF THE MEDDLERS

Gladys, the lady who served them breakfast, brought the tea and coffee to the Enquiry Room. She had added a bandage over her head like a hair band. It was not clear whether the white fabric was intended to be just that – a hair band – or a bandage. Either way it did not seem to be doing a great deal of good.

"That lady wore a bandage in her hair!" said Mr Tickle with a sudden bubble of laughter that was clearly threatening to burst over them all again at any moment.

Perhaps Bourne feared it might do just that, because he once more started the proceedings. As they enjoyed their tea and biscuits, the tale of the adventure continued from the point where Mr Tickle and Timmy and Jack had left the town of Topsy-Turvy, the subsequent long drive they had managed on the damaged Snow-Beater, and the details of the hours of that never-ending night.

"These boys were marvellous!" said Mr Tickle. "And this young man," he glanced admiringly at Timmy, "he looked after me, and calmed me down and seemed to know exactly what to do without being told! He deserves a medal! They both do!"

Jack was a bit embarrassed by Mr Tickle's glowing report, although he thought Timmy deserved everything Mr Tickle said about him.

"I don't deserve any of it," said Timmy frankly.

"You were great, Timmy," said Jack.

"No," said Timmy. "Not really. I'm just a broken Christian. I get things wrong all the time."

"I was broken," whispered Josie, "but the Lord Jesus made me a brand-new person. The same as you are, Timmy. Mended and whole in God's sight!"

"Amen," said Mr Tickle. And he patted Josie's hand.

"I know that," said Timmy. "But I seem to do so many wrong things. I don't know how a Christian should behave at all!"

Bourne and Mr Stable and Harold took Timmy very seriously. And Mrs Stable didn't comment on the distraction from the Rescuer Enquiry. She sat patiently with her stick poised above the screen, not writing anything at all.

"Every Christian is intended to represent the Lord Jesus on earth," said Mr Stable. "So, as much as possible, a Christian should be like the Lord Jesus."

"You see, God is so pleased with His Son, the Lord Jesus, He wants to see Christians as like Him as possible. And, one

day, He's going to fill Heaven with people just like His Son,"
said Bourne.

"Christian faith always directs us to a Person, and that is the Person
of the Lord Jesus," said Mr Stable. "It's not about dos and don'ts and
rules and regulations. It's about becoming as much like the Lord Jesus
as it is possible to be!"

"How can we be like the Lord Jesus?" asked Timmy. "I don't seem
to be able to improve myself at all!"

"This is a most important matter," said Mr Stable earnestly. "And
the first thing to understand is that you can't improve yourself."

"Can't he?" asked Josie.

"It's not just a problem with Timmy," said Bourne. "It's all of
us. The Bible teaches that there is absolutely nothing good inside
us[12]. And our old, sinful nature, and all the problems we have
in us – greed, pride, temper, lies, whatever it might be – are not
improved one tiny bit when we get saved, or even by a lifetime
of Christian living. We're not improved by religion, or riches,
or education, or therapy, or our environment, or any such
thing."

"We learned about that from Mr Tickle, after visiting Topsy-Turvy,"
said Jack, thinking that this, at least, was a good point in Mr Tickle's
favour.

"Yes, Topsy-Turvy is a good example of what happens when you focus on yourself and try and bring out goodness where there is no good," agreed Mr Stable.

"So, how can we become like the Lord Jesus?" prompted Josie.

"When you became a Christian, God made you a whole new creation in Christ Jesus[28]! It's not self improvement – because there's nothing in self that can be improved. Instead God has given you a brand-new nature which pleases Him and which can grow and develop and become like the Lord Jesus," explained Mr Stable.

"That's why the word *Christian* means *follower of Christ*," remarked Mrs Stable. "We're meant to be recognised as Christians because we're like the Lord Jesus Christ."

"When you were saved," continued Bourne, "God did not remove your old sinful nature. You don't get rid of that until you get to Heaven."

"So, until we go to Heaven, we live with *two* natures inside us," said Mr Stable. "One is the old, sinful nature that wants to do wrong things; and the other is the new nature that God gave us when we were saved. The old nature is just waiting to be encouraged and then BANG!" and Mr Stable thumped his hand hard on the table and made everybody jump and Mrs Stable drop her writing stick altogether. "Then, if we give the old nature any room, we go wrong and don't behave like a Christian should."

"Starve the old nature away until it's too weak to take over!" said Mr Tickle cheerfully.

"Starve it?" asked Timmy.

Mr Tickle nodded. "When I was young we were always taught that as a Christian *you are what you eat*! Of course, that doesn't mean real food like my good sausages!" and he chuckled with enjoyment at his little joke. "It means the things you take in from the world around you. Like things you think, and watch, and read, and do! You have to take in the right food, you see?"

"Just about anything I do will feed one or other of these two natures," said Harold. "The nature I appeal to the most – the old, sinful one, or the new one I receive as a Christian – will take over."

"The answer is to give no room to the old, sinful nature at all," said Bourne.

"Instead, fill yourself up by feeding the new nature God has given you,[29]" added Harold. "Then you will become more and more like the Lord Jesus, which is exactly what God wants you to be!"

"How exactly do you do that?" asked Jack.

"Read the Bible every day and pray always," said Harold. "That's the bread-and-butter of your new Christian diet."

"Think about practical, everyday things," said Bourne. "Like the friends you choose. If possible, make Christian friends who will encourage you to please God. They will help you feed on the right things."

"Think about the books you read," suggested Harold, "make sure they don't conflict with the teaching of the Bible; and the things you watch – if they make you feel uncomfortable then they are likely to be feeding your old, sinful nature, not the new nature that God intends should be like the Lord Jesus."

"The places you go," said Mr Stable. "Go to places where you know God can bless you and where you wouldn't be ashamed if the Lord Jesus came with you too. After all, you're meant to be representing Him in everything you do!"

"The Bible calls all of this walking by faith, not by sight,[6]" said Bourne. "It's a new kind of life, and a new kind of walk – that is, a new way of living – too."

Jack thought about everything the Lord Jesus had done when He died on the cross to set people free from their old, sinful natures so they could live a new life entirely. A life that represented Him! Why would people choose to feed on the wrong things that the Lord Jesus had died to save them from? Jack hoped he would remember to always feed on the right things. He hoped that he would be recognised as someone who represented the Lord Jesus on earth. What an important job that was!

At last they reached the part of the story where the Meddlers ended the valiant efforts of the Snow-Beater and the journey was completely broken. Jack and Timmy and Mr Tickle described the attack of the Red-Jacket Meddlers, the account of which went smoothly enough, with only one further outburst of unrestrained laughter from Mr Tickle. Until the tale was told to the Enquiry, Mr Tickle had not appreciated that the Red-Jacket Meddlers had, in the course of their destruction of the Snow-Beater, also destroyed the Christmas cake that Timmy was carrying to Jack's mum.

"Oh dear, oh dear!" Mr Tickle chortled, once more wiping tears of laughter from his eyes. "I'm not laughing at your mother losing her Christmas cake of course," he explained to Timmy, "it's just the thought of all those Christmas cake crumbs all over me! There might even be some raisins still in my hair under my thinking cap! Ha Ha!"

When Mr Tickle had his giggles under control, Jack and Timmy related how they had heard Josie's cry for help.

"I didn't know I cried for help," said Josie. "I prayed, of course, but I'm not sure I cried out loud for help!"

"We heard it anyway," said Timmy. After all their strange experiences in Err neither of the boys was inclined to question Josie's account of things. Perhaps God alone had directed them to her.

"I thought I was going to die," said Josie. "I lay down beside that awful pond and saw once and for all how completely broken I was."

"I thought she was dead," Jack said solemnly.

"Dear me," murmured Sanny, busy recording details with her stick.

Josie explained that she had run away from the Mending Centre about the time that Jack and Timmy were reaching Plod's shelter. She went through the streets of Broken looking for the home of Melody, the movie star she had idolised. Err-Vision reported that Melody had left the town of Celebrity and moved to Broken. It was a big scandal. The once beautiful, rich and successful movie star had lost all she had and ended up in a town where everything was broken. Josie couldn't believe it. She wanted to be just like Melody and she couldn't imagine how anyone who had everything Josie imagined would make you completely happy could end up in Broken. She had begged to go on the Christmas mission; she had behaved so well that her parents let her go with the Wallops.

But Josie's plan, she confessed, had only ever been to search for Melody.

Josie found Melody. The movie star was wrapped in bandages, living in a tumbledown house, completely without hope. In utter horror, Josie ran away. Seeing Melody like that was the end of all her dreams about what would make her happy. She wanted to get away from Broken and go somewhere else in Err where there were truly happy people who had everything. She didn't plan or think about anything but getting away. She left the town and began struggling across the snowfields of Err.

"Will we be able to help Melody?" asked Josie.

"We'll certainly try," said Bourne.

"I've visited her," said Sanny. "We'll keep working and praying for her, dear."

Josie wasn't far from Broken when she came across a very strange shelter in the forlorn landscape of snow and broken things.

"It was really weird," she said. "Like a massive tree trunk had fallen down, the way that most of the branches seem to. It was huge! Taller than me. And I think I saw a door in the end of the tree trunk – a real door that people could go through and shelter!"

"Did you take shelter there?" asked Bourne.

Josie shook her head. "I wanted to," she said. "I wanted to shelter somewhere and hide away. But I heard voices; nasty, cold voices. They were talking about horrible things."

Jack noticed that Mr Stable and Bourne and Harold were suddenly paying avid attention.

"What were they talking about?" asked Mr Stable.

"They were talking about Aletheia," said Josie.

"Meddlers!" murmured Harold.

"I don't think so," said Josie slowly. "They didn't talk like the ones that attacked me later in Fracture Wood, when I found the pond. Those Meddlers spoke in silly voices and muddled their words. They behaved like spoilt children, only a lot more dangerous. They pelted me with dirty snowballs with stones in them and made me despair that I would ever, ever be mended!"

Mr Tickle patted Josie's hand. "The rascals!" he murmured indignantly. "They don't know the greatness and power of the Lord Jesus, eh?"

"No, they don't," agreed Josie with a radiant smile. However awful her experience had been, it was all blotted out in the wonder that she was saved: made whole forever. "But the voices I heard in the tree trunk didn't sound like those Meddlers."

"Blue-Stocking Meddlers perhaps?" Mr Stable murmured to Bourne.

"That's what I'm thinking," said Bourne. "Now, Josie, think carefully."

"And Sanny, you must note this carefully," said Mr Stable.

"I always note things carefully, Welly," said Sanny. "As you very well know!"

"What exactly was being discussed in the hollow tree trunk?" asked Bourne. "Try to remember any small detail you can, any words, no matter how unimportant it might seem."

"I think they called what they were discussing Phase One," said Josie, screwing up her face and trying to remember. "I'm afraid I didn't care about any of the details at the time, I only wanted to get away from everything!"

"That's alright," said Bourne, "just tell us everything you can."

"Well, this Phase One, or whatever it was, was to do with weakening Aletheia. 'Take away their power,' I heard one of them say."

Bourne leaned forward anxiously over the table. "Prayer," he said urgently. "Did they mention prayer?"

Josie shut her eyes tight and tried her best to recall the strange and unexpected conversation she had heard in a tree trunk in the middle of her frantic flight. "I don't know," she said with a sigh. "I'm sorry, I don't know. But they said 'their power'; they definitely used the word *power.*"

"Never mind," said Mr Stable, concern creasing his brow, "that's very helpful. What else did you hear? What else did they say?"

"Don't rush her, Welly," said Sanny, tapping quickly with her stick. "You take your time, dear."

"There was something about the 'tall tower'," said Josie. "'Power-tower', I think they called it, but I've never heard of that in Aletheia."

"The Prayer Academy," murmured Harold. "The highest tower in Aletheia!"

Bourne nodded. "It *is* about prayer," he muttered.

They all looked terribly concerned.

"A Care-Caster?" said Josie hesitantly. "I know that sounds unlikely, but..."

"Not at all unlikely, young lady," said Mr Stable eagerly. "What did they say about the Care-Caster?"

"She's just about to tell you, Welly, if you give her a chance," said Sanny calmly.

"Imagine them knowing about the Care-Caster!" murmured Harold, clearly appalled.

"'Keep them fishing'," said Josie, clearly puzzled. "They said 'keep them fishing'. I remember those bits because I thought I'd quite like to see a Care-Caster – whatever it is – and cast all my cares inside it! And I remembered the fishing bit because it just sounded so, uh, weird."

"Quite," said Bourne tightly.

"They had a silly rhyme," said Josie. "I only remember the first bit, 'Fretters for the Old, Distractions for the Young'. I'm sorry, I can't remember the rest."

"Are you sure you can't remember the rest?" urged Mr Stable. "Anything at all about the rest of the rhyme?"

"Really, Welly," began Mrs Stable, but Timmy surprised them all by interrupting with, "Fretters for the Old,

> Distractions for the Young,
>
> Issues for the In-Betweens,
>
> Our Plan have we begun!"

Josie stared at him. "That's it!" she said. "I forgot the rest! How did you learn it?"

"We heard it in Fracture Wood," said Jack.

"The Red-Jacket Meddlers were chanting it," said Timmy. "It all sounded very silly."

"Silly indeed," said Bourne grimly.

"The Red-Jackets must have infiltrated the Blue-Stockings and learned their plan," said Harold. "They probably don't have a clue what they're repeating!"

"The Red-Jackets are too simple to understand a plan such as the Blue-Stockings could put together," agreed Mr Stable. "We must be very thankful we have received this vital intelligence!"

"Is it very serious?" asked Josie.

"About as serious as it can be," said Mr Stable. "And we must thank God that He placed you young people in just the right place so at least we're forewarned!"

"We'll need to notify the Chief as soon as possible," said Bourne.

"I could take a Capsule to Aletheia tonight," said Harold. He had recently gained his flying licence and was eager to use it as much as possible.

"I think that's a good idea," said Mr Stable. "You can meet with the Chief in person."

"But what does it mean?" asked Josie. "Is Aletheia in danger?"

Bourne nodded. "Yes," he said sadly.

Mr Stable looked stern and grim. "It means the Meddlers have learned the source of our power," he said. "They're going to target *prayer!*"

The Rescuer Enquiry drew to an abrupt close. There were no serious consequences for Mr Tickle. Afterwards the children privately agreed that this was probably due to the concern of the panel members at the plan of the Meddlers. Bourne and Harold and the Stables met with the other Rescuer staff at the Mending Centre. They were closeted in the Rescuer Enquiry Room long after the children and Mr Tickle had left it.

"An attack on Aletheia!" exclaimed Henrietta as they all guessed at the details the adults were discussing.

"I wonder what the Meddlers could do to Aletheia," said Josie. In the past she hadn't really liked Aletheia; but now that she had seen the Truth it was a precious place to her.

"I wonder how they stop people praying," said Hugo.

"I hope we can all help if there is an attack," said Hezekiah.

The children had no answers to their questions about the plan of the Meddlers. And when Harold joined them it was not to satisfy their curiosity. He was flying to Aletheia to brief the Chief of the Rescuers about the Meddlers' plans, and with him would be three witnesses. Jack and Timmy and Josie would be returning to the city of Aletheia.

"Do you want to wear your watch, Jack?" asked Hezekiah anxiously. He had great faith in the powers of Jack's spy watch to help in an emergency.

"That's alright, Zek," said Jack. "You might need it too. You keep it until I get back."

CHAPTER 19
FLIGHT TO ALETHEIA

The Rescue Capsule stood on long, sturdy legs above the mounds of broken, misshapen snow.

"We're flying Capsule Three-Twenty-Three," said Harold. "We should make Aletheia inside of two hours, avoiding the storms."

"Gladys, the broken lady, gave me cookies for the journey," said Josie as they walked across and around the mounds of snow to the Capsule steps. She peered into the bag of cookies that Gladys had kindly bestowed. "Oh! They're all broken!" she said.

"I think I could have guessed that," said Timmy drily.

Josie giggled.

"I expect they still taste the same," said Jack. He seemed to feel perpetually hungry; he figured he was still making up for the long, hungry hours on their broken journey. He didn't care whether the cookies were broken or not.

Harold started the soft, whirring engines of Capsule Three-Twenty-Three, and Jack followed Josie and Timmy up the steps into it.

He hesitated for a moment before he entered the door. Perched on the steps he could see into the next street of Broken where someone was trying to clear a path through the snow. They had a bandage around the handle of the spade they used, and one on each hand too. Jack hoped that the Christmas mission in Broken could continue despite the threat to Aletheia. He hoped the bandaged man slowly digging snow with a bandaged spade would learn about the Lord Jesus coming into the world to bring peace and healing to broken people.

Jack clambered aboard the Capsule.

It was darker than he anticipated; the light inside the main cabin faded swiftly and strangely to almost nothing at all.

"Timmy?"

There was no sound of anyone.

And, as Jack's eyes adjusted to the dimness around him, he experienced the biggest surprise of all.

Jack didn't know how long he stood still and silent in the attic. Probably it was not too long, and he wondered if any time at all had passed since he had last stood here, since he had made his way through the door in the wall. There was still a door there and Jack opened it cautiously, holding his breath. There was a small cupboard behind the door. It contained large, mysterious shapes covered by sheets and blankets. He had, at last, discovered the hiding place of the Christmas presents. He didn't take a closer look. It no longer seemed as important as before. He quietly closed the cupboard door and spotted a pair of old boots on some shelves – very much like the ones he had seen here before. But there were no longer dozens of pairs: only one scruffy pair in solitary splendour in the dust.

He stepped out of the attic, switched off the light, and shut the door behind him.

"Jack?" Mum was calling. "Jack? Are you up there?"

"Coming!" called Jack.

Mum looked at him slightly suspiciously when Jack appeared in the kitchen, out of breath from his run down the stairs. "I hope you haven't been anywhere you shouldn't," she said.

Jack wondered what Mum would say if she knew exactly where he had been. He might tell his younger brother, Harris, about it. Harris enjoyed his stories about the land of Err.

"That was Timmy's mum on the phone," explained Mum. "He's away for a few days so unfortunately he won't be able to make it to your Christmas party."

"Oh!" said Jack. And he had a very strange, very weird thought. Perhaps, just perhaps, Timmy was still in the land of Err. Maybe Timmy would attend the meeting with the Chief Rescuer and help explain about the plan of the Meddlers.

Mum gave Jack a strange look. "Are you alright about Timmy not coming to your party, Jack?" she asked kindly.

"Oh yes," said Jack.

"Timmy's mum said she baked us a Christmas cake that Timmy was meant to give you," said Mum.

"Oh," said Jack.

"Oh, Jack," sighed Mum. "I don't suppose even you could lose a whole Christmas cake?"

"Not exactly *lose*," said Jack.

He wasn't sure how he would explain its whereabouts and the adventure that had befallen that particular Christmas cake. But Jack was not one to worry unduly about things that were unexplainable.

There was only one further anomaly arising from the adventure that Jack was also unable to explain.

"I'm going to give that old blanket of my grandmother's to Aunt Bess for Christmas," Jack overheard his mum say to his dad. "It's only taking up space in the attic, after all."

"Did someone die in the blanket?" asked Jack.

"Die in the blanket?!" exclaimed Mum. "Jack, you really do have the most extraordinary ideas!"

Jack was uncertain whether that meant the story of the death in the blanket was true, or not. He was rather inclined to think it was, and Harris certainly believed it.

But the ghosts of the quilt had certainly been laid to rest in Jack's mind. He liked to think of that blanket now. Poor Aunt Bess would certainly never receive it. Instead, the faded, knitted patches and the musty scent belonged to another person entirely: to a kind boy Jack liked to think of as his friend. A boy named Dusty Addle. He hoped the blanket might bring Dusty comfort if the Meddlers really did attack Aletheia.

Jack thought of the plan of the Meddlers. It was Christmas, the time of peace and plenty. But how long would the city of Aletheia, the city of the Truth, remain at peace?

A storm was gathering on the horizon.

Aletheia was under threat.

EPILOGUE

They met behind closed doors, deep in the secure fortress which was the Academy of Soldiers-of-the-Cross. The Chief Rescuer of the land of Err, Chief Steadfast, was seated at the head of the table. Not only was he the Chief of the Rescuers, he was ultimately in charge of the whole of Aletheia. He was a massive man with broad shoulders and grey hair. His face was lined with cares, scarred by battles, and wise with experience. His son, Captain Ready Steadfast, Deputy Chief Rescuer, sat at his right hand. The long table was lined with other senior Rescuers: experienced men and women with gold stripes on their shoulders and medals on their uniforms. They were battle-wise, prayer-burdened, Truth-endowed.

Sprinkled throughout the Rescuers were others in different attire. They represented the other responsibilities in the city of Aletheia. There was Mr Hardy Wallop, Superintendent of Entry to Aletheia; Mr Roger Stalwart, Director of the Prayer Academy; Mr Philologus Mustardpot, Head of Education; Miss Sagacia Steady, Chief Judge; Mrs Tranquil Serene, Manager of the Run-the-Race Retirement Home; Miss Candour Communique, Chief Editor of *The Truth* newspaper; Mr Sturdy Wright, Head Keeper of the Water of Sound Doctrine; Dr Theo Pentone,

Director of Health, and other smart-suited, official-looking managers besides.

Looking self-conscious and not a little sheepish, halfway down the company of the great and the good of Aletheia, was Mr Croft Straw. He was introduced as "the representative of Pray-Always Farmlands", refusing any grander title. He was only there because none of the farmers enjoyed 'official' meetings and it was his turn to act as their representative. Whilst he had great affection and respect for those seated around him, he felt awkward in his best tweed suit and was wondering whether his tie covered in pictures of cows had been the most suitable choice for this auspicious occasion. He fiddled with the cap in his huge hands; with the tie at his neck; and lastly with the coffee cup in front of him – until the dainty china handle broke and then he just sat on his hands altogether.

"Never mind," whispered Candour Communique who was sitting next to him, and when he wasn't looking she kindly swapped their cups. She had tried in vain to write an article on the summer blight that had affected the Pray-Always farms but had made absolutely no inroads with shy Mr Straw. She was still hoping he would change his mind about an interview.

Harold Wallop, without any gold stripes or medals on his Rescuer uniform, was seated at the end of the long line of Rescuer warriors and heroes. He would not usually have attended a meeting of such seniority and experience, but he was a link to the first occasion the city of Aletheia had been alerted to the dastardly plan of the Meddlers: alerted through the strange events of a broken journey undertaken by three children and one bumbling old man. Seated by Harold was his cousin and comrade, Lieutenant Bourne Faithful. Bourne was glowering. He didn't like official meetings either, no matter how necessary they might be. He preferred action.

Beyond the thick stone walls of the Academy the wind howled and the winter snowstorms continued unabated. No one present at that meeting could remember such a winter in Aletheia; none could remember such a threat.

"We now understand the Blue-Stocking Meddlers have been secretly studying and beginning to undermine our use of prayer for some time," said the Chief. "The Blue-Stocking Meddlers are cunning and evidently cleverer than we have previously experienced."

"How is it we didn't even know they were interested in attacking prayer?" asked a senior Rescuer.

"They've been working with Sloths," said the Chief, "directing them to encourage idleness and apathy amongst a large percentage of our praying population. They have been working with other creatures in Err too. However, that does not excuse us. We should have been on the alert. The Pray-Always farms have suffered an unusual blight this summer. Mr Straw, would you care to comment on this?"

Mr Straw certainly did *not* care to comment on this. He cleared his throat and went bright red. "Uh, it's just as you say," he said. "We reported the blight because, uh, because it was unusually severe. It seemed to us to mean, uh, a problem with prayer."

"Thank you, Mr Straw," said the Chief. "It was faithfully reported by the Pray-Always farms, and we at the Academy missed the sign of a problem approaching!"

There were murmurs up and down the table and Mr Straw once more fiddled with the coffee cup and nearly broke another handle. Candour Communique removed it from his reach when he wasn't looking.

"But at least we have early warning of the first phase of the Meddlers' attack," said Captain Steadfast. "We must consider how to counter the attack that is now inevitable and may already – judging by the harsh weather – be underway."

There were more quiet murmurs of concern amongst those gathered.

"You have all heard the Meddlers' rhyme by now," said the Chief.

"Fretters for the Old,

Distractions for the Young,

> Issues for the In-Betweens,
>
> Our Plan have we begun!"

"The rhyme may sound silly," continued Captain Steadfast, "but we believe it summarises the strategy used by the Meddlers to target our prayer power and overthrow the Truth. It was probably intended to be kept secret but was spread by the lower orders of Meddlers who were annoyed at being excluded from the Blue-Stockings' secret discussions."

"We already know that Fretters are being multiplied by the Meddlers and will be released to target some of our greatest prayer warriors at the Run-the-Race Retirement Home. As you know, Fretters can spread illness or cause fretting over health, or families, or other issues. The result they wish for is that people will not pray effectively," said the Chief. "Have you noticed any effect on our reliable prayer warriors, Tranquil?"

Mrs Tranquil Serene nodded soberly. "A slight, but noticeable, increase in anxiety, depression, and some illness," she said.

"We have noticed a downturn – slight as yet – in the prayer cover we usually receive from the Retirement Home," said Roger Stalwart of the Prayer Academy.

The Chief glanced at Dr Theo Pentone, the Director of Health. "Noticeable increase in admissions to our wards due to fretting-type illnesses," confirmed the doctor.

There were yet more murmurs of concern from around the room. The Meddlers' plan had already commenced, right in the heart of the city of the Truth.

"The young will be distracted by whatever the Meddlers can get onto Err-Vision and into the city," continued Captain Steadfast. "This is not a new tactic, but we think they will be launching something specific to distract our young Christians away from prayer. Philologus, this will be one to keep an eye on in the schools."

"You'll have both my eyes, my ears, and my mind on it!" promised the formidable Mr Philologus Mustardpot in his booming voice.

"The 'Issues for the In-Betweens' is more unknown," said the Chief. "This is the main adult age-group and makes up our largest group of Christians and biggest prayer source. At this stage we feel this attack will initially target The Outskirts of Aletheia, where adults are more vulnerable to distraction because they live away from the cross."

"We also know, thanks to our early sources, that targeting the Care-Caster at the Prayer Academy is part of the Meddlers' plan to destroy prayer," added Captain Steadfast.

There were louder murmurs of concern. If people didn't learn to cast their cares properly, they would spend all their time worrying about them – instead of praying for other things!

"So, what's our plan, Chief?" asked Mr Mustardpot in his best Headmaster's voice. "We must do something!"

The Chief nodded. "We shall certainly do something," he said firmly. "That is exactly what we must do now: come up with a plan of defence! Now, where shall we begin?"

It was the start of the plan for the defence of Aletheia.

For the attack of the Meddlers had already begun.

REFERENCES

Unless otherwise stated, all Bible references are taken from the New King James Version of the Bible.

1.   [References on pages 8, 23, 33, 51, 79, 99] You can read about this adventure in Book 1 of the Aletheia Adventure Series, The Rescue of Timmy Trial.

2.   [References on pages 22, 59] When the Lord Jesus was on earth He healed many people and made them whole from many sicknesses and diseases. This is also a picture of how He can save people from all the damage caused by sin and make them whole again. An example of a verse about this is:

Mark 6:56:

"And as many as touched Him [the Lord Jesus] were made whole."

[King James Version]

3.   [References on pages 26, 47] The Bible talks about Christians putting on the 'armour of God'. This is explained in:

Ephesians 6:10-18:

"Finally, my brethren, be strong in the Lord and in the power of His might.

Put on the whole armour of God, that you may be able to stand against the wiles of the devil. For we do not wrestle against flesh and blood, but against principalities, against powers, against the rulers of the darkness of this age, against spiritual hosts of wickedness in the heavenly places. Therefore take up the whole armour of God, that you may be able to withstand in the evil day, and having done all, to stand.

Stand therefore, having girded your waist with truth, having put on the breastplate of righteousness, and having shod your feet with the preparation of the gospel of peace; above all, taking the shield of faith with which you will be able to quench all the fiery darts of the wicked one. And take the helmet of salvation, and the sword of the Spirit, which is the word of God; praying always with all prayer and supplication in the Spirit..."

4. [References on pages 26, 129] This is a reference to:

Ephesians 6:17:

"And take...the sword of the Spirit, which is the word of God."

(Also see reference 3 above which explains about all of the armour of God).

5. [Reference on page 27] The Lord Jesus came to earth to offer peace to people. Here are some Bible references about this:

John 14:27:

[The Lord Jesus is speaking] "Peace I leave with you, My peace I give to you; not as the world gives do I give to you. Let not your heart be troubled, neither let it be afraid."

Romans 5:1:

"Therefore, having been justified by faith, we have peace with God through our Lord Jesus Christ."

Ephesians 2:14:

"For He Himself [the Lord Jesus] is our peace."

6. [References on pages 40, 192] There is a verse about this in:

2 Corinthians 5:7:

"For we walk by faith, not by sight."

7. [Reference on page 65] There are verses in the Bible that show that once someone has trusted in the Lord Jesus, they are saved forever. For example:

John 10:28-29:

"And I give them eternal life, and they shall never perish; neither shall anyone snatch them out of My hand. My Father, who has given them to Me, is greater than all; and no one is able to snatch them out of My Father's hand."

John 5:24:

[The Lord Jesus speaking] "Most assuredly, I say to you, he who hears My word and believes in Him who sent Me has everlasting life, and shall not come into judgment but has passed from death into life."

John 6:47:

[The Lord Jesus speaking] "Most assuredly, I say to you, he who believes in Me has everlasting life."

8. [Reference on page 66] The Bible is spoken of as a light to show us the way. This is a reference to:

    Psalm 119:105:

    "Your word is a lamp to my feet

    And a light to my path."

    [This doesn't mean that the Bible is a literal light; this verse is saying that the Word of God will be our guide through life if we believe what it says.]

9. [Reference on page 77] This is a quote from:

    Isaiah 26:3:

"You will keep him in perfect peace,

Whose mind is stayed on You,

Because he trusts in You."

10.   [Reference on page 78] This is a quote from:

Proverbs 20:3:

"It is honourable for a man to stop striving,

Since any fool can start a quarrel [or be a meddler]."

11.   [Reference on page 79] The Bible teaches that if we sin as

Christians, we can confess our sin and God will forgive us.

1 John 1:9:

"If we confess our sins, He is faithful and just to forgive us our

sins and to cleanse us from all unrighteousness."

12.   [References on pages 119, 120, 143, 189] The Bible teaches that

everyone has sinned, and that the reason we sin is that we are

fundamentally wrong inside, and have been so ever since Adam

sinned in the Garden of Eden and sin entered into the world.

The Bible often calls the inside part of a person – the part that

thinks, and plans, and feels – the heart.

Jeremiah 17:9:

"The heart is deceitful above all things,

And desperately wicked;

Who can know it?"

13. [Reference on page 119] The Bible teaches that sin entered into the world when Adam and Eve sinned in the Garden of Eden. You can read the account of this in **Genesis chapter 3**. There are also verses in the New Testament that explain the consequences of Adam's sin for all of mankind. You can read about this in **Romans chapter 5**.

14. [Reference on page 119] There are many verses in the Bible that show how people can be saved and made right with God. Here are some examples:

John 3:16:

"For God so loved the world that He gave His only begotten Son, that whoever believes in Him should not perish but have everlasting life."

Romans 8:1:

"There is therefore now no condemnation to those who are in Christ Jesus."

Romans 10:9:

"That if you confess with your mouth the Lord Jesus and believe in your heart that God has raised Him from the dead, you will be saved."

15. [Reference on page 120] 'Sin' is the Bible name for all the wrong things that everyone has done. The Bible teaches that everyone has sinned [done wrong things] against God and broken his laws. **Romans 3:23**:

"For all have sinned and fall short of the glory of God."

16. [Reference on page 120] The Bible teaches that believing in the Lord Jesus is the only way to be saved and made right with God. A couple of verses that explain this are:

1 Timothy 2:5:

"For there is one God and one Mediator between God and men, the Man Christ Jesus."

John 14:6:

"Jesus said to him, "I am the way, the truth, and the life. No one comes to the Father except through Me."

17. [References on pages 128, 142] The Bible teaches that the sacrifice of the Lord Jesus, when He shed His blood at the cross,

can cleanse from every sin that we ever commit if we confess our sin to God. There is a verse about this in:

1 John 1:7:

"And the blood of Jesus Christ His [God's] Son cleanses us from all sin."

18. [Reference on page 128] This verse can be found in:

2 Corinthians 12:9:

"And He [God] said to me, "My grace is sufficient for you, for My strength is made perfect in weakness.""

19. [Reference on page 128] This is a quote from a verse which is found in:

Romans 7:18:

"For I know that in me (that is, in my flesh) nothing good dwells."

20. [Reference on page 129] The description "living and powerful Word of God" comes from:

Hebrews 4:12:

"For the word of God is living and powerful, and sharper than any two-edged sword, piercing even to the division of soul and spirit, and of joints and marrow, and is a discerner of the thoughts and intents of the heart."

21. [Reference on page 142] There is a passage in the Bible that teaches about what it means to be "born again": see **John 3: 3 – 8.**

22. [Reference on page 143] The Bible teaches that no one is right before God. We all need to trust in the Lord Jesus to be made right. There is a verse about this in:

Romans 3:10:

"There is none righteous, no, not one."

23. [Reference on page 144] The Bible shows that the Lord Jesus came to pay the price for the sins of the whole world. However, only people who trust in Him will have their sins taken away. Here are examples of verses that teach about this:

John 1:29:

"John saw Jesus coming toward him, and said, "Behold! The Lamb of God who takes away the sin of the world!""

John 3:16:

"For God so loved the world that He gave His only begotten

Son, that whoever believes in Him should not perish but have everlasting life."

24. [Reference on page 152] When someone becomes a Christian the angels rejoice.

Luke 15:10:

"Likewise, I say to you, there is joy in the presence of the angels of God over one sinner who repents."

25. [Reference on page 166] The Bible makes it clear that the Lord Jesus came to seek and save people. You can read about this in:

Luke 19:10:

"For the Son of Man has come to seek and to save that which was lost."

26. [Reference on page 167] You can read about this adventure, when Jack left his spy watch in Aletheia, in Book 2 of the Aletheia Adventure Series, The Purple Storm.

27. [Reference on page 169] The Bible teaches that when we have confessed our sins to God and trusted in the Lord Jesus, our sins are forgiven and completely blotted out. That means, as

far as God is concerned, that they don't exist anymore. For example:

Psalm 103:12:

"As far as the east is from the west,

So far has He removed our transgressions from us."

Acts 3:19:

"Repent therefore and be converted, that your sins may be blotted out."

Isaiah 44:22:

"I have blotted out, like a thick cloud, your transgressions,

And like a cloud, your sins."

Jeremiah 31:34:

"For I [God] will forgive their iniquity, and their sin I will remember no more."

28. [Reference on page 190] The Bible teaches that when someone becomes a Christian they have a new life. This doesn't mean that the old person is improved, but it means that God has given a completely different kind of life to someone who is saved; they have been "born again" (John 3:3).

A verse which illustrates this is:

2 Corinthians 5:17:

"Therefore, if anyone is in Christ, he is a new creation; old things have passed away; behold, all things have become new."

29. [Reference on page 191] There are verses in the Bible that use food and drink to illustrate that a Christian should desire to 'feed' on the right things in order to grow in the right way. For example:

1 Peter 2:2:

"As newborn babes, desire the pure milk of the word, that you may grow thereby."